Cook It Light

DESSERTS

The Calculating Cook 1972

Diet for a Happy Heart 1975

Secrets of Salt-Free Cooking 1979

The Canyon Ranch Cookbook 1984

Cook It Light 1987

Eating Smart 1991

Jeanne Jones Entertains 1992

Cook It Light Classics 1992

Cook It Light Pasta, Rice, and Beans 1994

Light and Hearty 1994

Cook It Light

DESSERTS

Jeanne Jones

MACMILLAN • USA

This book is dedicated with deep appreciation
to the millions of people who read my column,
"Cook It Light," each week. Your letters are a constant
source of challenge and inspiration for everything I do.

MACMILLAN
A Prentice Hall Macmillan Company
15 Columbus Circle
New York, NY 10023

Library of Congress Cataloging-in-Publication Data
Jones, Jeanne.
Cook it light desserts / Jeanne Jones.
p.   cm.
Includes index.
ISBN 0-02-559774-4
1. Desserts.   2. Low-fat diet—Recipes.   3. Low-calorie diet—Recipes.
I. Title.
TX773.J69   1994
641.8'6—dc20   94-2219
                                                        CIP

Manufactured in the United States of America

10 9 8 7 6 5 4 3 2 1

Designed by Laura Hammond Hough

Contents

Acknowledgments

In grateful acknowledgment: Julie Segal, nutritional analysis; Tracy DeMas, recipe development and testing; William Hansen, organization of manuscript; Margaret McBride, my agent; Pam Hoenig, my editor; Justin Schwartz, assistance.

Introduction

I receive thousands of letters each year from my readers asking me to revise their favorite recipes so that they are lower in calories, fat, cholesterol, and sodium. Twenty-five percent of these requests are for sweets and desserts.

For this reason, I decided to devote an entire book to this obviously popular category. The recipes in this book which I originally designed for spa menus are extremely low in both calories and fat. Others are revisions of very high calorie desserts and, while these recipes are much lighter than the original versions, they are certainly not spartan.

There are times when I simply cannot appreciably change the nutritional profile of a really rich dessert without totally destroying the integrity of the original recipe. In these cases, I suggest to my readers to use moderation by making the recipe infrequently and eating less of it when they do. I am a firm believer in the enjoyment of really good food, and I think it is better, and more satisfying, to have a bite of something truly wonderful than a whole plateful of some "make do" dish.

My goal in writing this book was to have every recipe so delicious and satisfying that no one would ever guess it was a revision or a fake copy of some real "gem." I don't think we should ever have to apologize for a dessert by saying it is certainly good considering it is so low in calories and fat. It should be able to stand on its own as simply "delicious."

Fruit Desserts

The healthiest and certainly the easiest sweet snack or dessert is a piece of fresh fruit. However, there are times when we want to add a little pizzazz and variety to our fruit desserts and that is the exact purpose of this chapter.

Whether you want to do something as simple as Frozen Grapes (page 18) or as showy as making a fresh Fruit Gazpacho (page 6), I am sure that you will find these recipes helpful, inspiring, and fun.

Mango Soup with Almond Jelly

In China dessert soups are called "sweet water" and are very popular. The actual soup is usually nothing more than sugar dissolved in boiling water, or quite literally, sweet water, with fruit floating in it. I prefer both the taste and texture of this soup with part of the mango pureed and mixed with the "sweet water."

FOR THE ALMOND JELLY

1 envelope unflavored gelatin
¼ cup cool water
¼ cup boiling water
1 tablespoon sugar
1¼ cups nonfat milk
1 teaspoon pure almond extract

FOR THE SOUP

2 cups water
2 tablespoons sugar
4 cups chilled peeled, pitted, and diced fresh mango
Fresh mint sprigs for garnish (optional)

1. Stir the gelatin into the cool water and allow to soften. Add boiling water and stir until the gelatin is completely dissolved. Add the sugar and stir until it is dissolved. Add the milk and extract and mix well. Pour the mixture into a standard-size loaf pan. Cover tightly and refrigerate until firm, about 2 hours. When firm, unmold the jelly onto a cutting board and cut into ½-inch cubes. Place the cubes in a covered container and refrigerate until ready to use.

2. To make the soup, combine the water and sugar in a saucepan. Bring to a boil to dissolve the sugar. Remove from the heat and allow to come to room temperature. Place 2 cups of the mango in a blender and puree. Press through a fine strainer to remove any pulp, place in a bowl, and add the sugar water. Mix well and refrigerate until cold.

3. To serve, add the cubes of almond jelly and the remaining 2 cups of diced mango to the soup. Spoon the soup into 6 chilled bowls. Garnish with mint sprigs, if desired.

MAKES 6 GENEROUS 1-CUP SERVINGS

*Each serving contains approximately: Calories: 127;
Grams of fat: negligible; Cholesterol: 1 mg; Sodium: 29 mg*

Minted Melon Soup

I originally developed this recipe for *Cooking Healthy* magazine as the first course for a Sunday brunch menu. This brilliantly beautiful and refreshing cold melon soup is also a wonderfully light summer dessert.

1 cup water
1 tablespoon sugar
1 bunch fresh mint, including stems
2 fresh basil leaves
1½ cups seeded and diced cantaloupe
4 teaspoons fresh lemon juice
1½ cups seeded and diced watermelon
4 fresh mint sprigs for garnish

1. Combine the water and sugar in a small saucepan and mix well. Bring to a boil over medium heat. Add the mint and basil and simmer over low heat until the liquid is reduced by two thirds, about 5 minutes. Remove from the heat and allow to stand for at least 2 hours. Strain the liquid and set aside.

2. Place the cantaloupe in a blender and puree. Add 2 tablespoons of the minted liquid and 2 teaspoons of the lemon juice and mix well. Pour into a container with a tight-fitting lid and refrigerate until cold.

3. Place the watermelon in the blender and follow the instructions in step 2.

4. To serve, pour ¼ cup of each melon soup into a bowl at the same time, one on one side and one on the other. Place a mint sprig in the center where the two colors meet.

MAKES FOUR ½-CUP SERVINGS

Each serving contains approximately: Calories: 64;
Grams of fat: negligible; Cholesterol: 0; Sodium: 8 mg

Cold Blueberry Soup

This is a recipe that I developed for the Canyon Ranch Fitness Resort in Tucson, Arizona, about ten years ago and it is still one of my favorite light desserts. I like to top each serving with a small scoop of pineapple sherbet and a sprig of fresh mint.

½ cup frozen unsweetened pineapple juice concentrate
½ cup water
1 teaspoon fresh lemon juice
3 cups fresh or thawed frozen unsweetened blueberries

1. Combine the concentrate, water, and lemon juice in a blender. Add 2 cups of the blueberries and puree.

2. Combine the pureed mixture with the remaining blueberries and mix well. Cover and refrigerate until cold before serving.

3. To serve, spoon ½ cup of the cold soup into each of six bowls. Spoon a small scoop of pineapple sherbet on the top, if desired.

MAKES SIX ½-CUP SERVINGS

Each serving contains approximately: Calories: 82;
Grams of fat: negligible; Cholesterol: 0; Sodium: 1 mg

Fruit Gazpacho

It is hard to believe that this exotically beautiful and delicious fresh fruit gazpacho is as healthy as it is impressive. It was created by Christian Rassinoux, the executive chef at the famous Ritz Carlton Resort in Laguna Niguel, California, for their Terrace Restaurant. I ordered it just because I was fascinated by the idea of making gazpacho out of fruit and serving it as dessert. When it arrived I was so impressed with both the presentation and the fabulous flavor that I asked if I could have the recipe to share with my readers. Now we can all surprise our guests with this sensational soup for dessert.

> *2 cups water*
> *½ cup sugar*
> *8 fresh mint sprigs*
> *2 fresh basil leaves*
> *4 cups fresh strawberries*
> *2 cups fresh raspberries*
> *2 tablespoons fresh lemon juice*
> *1 mango, peeled, pitted, and diced, for garnish*
> *1 papaya, peeled, seeded, and diced, for garnish*
> *2 kiwi, peeled and cut into julienne strips, for garnish*
> *Additional seasonal fresh fruits for garnish (optional)*

1. Combine the water and sugar in a small saucepan and heat over medium heat, stirring constantly, until the sugar has completely dissolved. Remove from the heat and allow to cool.

2. Remove the lower leaves from the mint sprigs (approximately 16 leaves), reserving the mint florets for garnish. Finely chop the mint leaves and basil and set aside.

3. Put 3 cups of the strawberries in a blender. Cut the remaining cup of strawberries into julienne strips and set aside. Add the raspberries and lemon juice to the strawberries in the blender and puree. Press the mixture through a fine strainer to remove the seeds. Add the chopped mint and basil and sugar water and mix well. Chill thoroughly before serving.

4. To serve, pour the soup into eight chilled bowls and garnish with the reserved strawberries, the mango, papaya, and kiwi. Top each serving with a mint sprig and other seasonal fresh fruits, if desired.

MAKES ABOUT EIGHT ¾-CUP SERVINGS OF THE SOUP WITHOUT GARNISH

> *Each serving contains approximately: Calories: 195;*
> *Grams of fat: negligible; Cholesterol: 0; Sodium: 4 mg*

Fresh Fruit Compote

¾ cup nonfat plain yogurt
1 small banana, peeled and sliced
1 small orange, peeled cleanly, seeded, and diced
1 cup diced fresh pineapple or pineapple chunks packed in natural
juice, drained

1. Put the yogurt and banana in a blender and blend until smooth. Set aside.

2. Combine the diced orange and pineapple. Place ⅓ cup of the mixture in a consommé cup and top with ¼ cup of the sauce.

Variation:

Any other fresh fruit may be substituted for the orange and pineapple.

MAKES FOUR ⅓-CUP SERVINGS

Each serving contains approximately: Calories: 91;
Grams of fat: negligible; Cholesterol: 1 mg; Sodium: 33 mg

Fantasy in Fruit

This dessert has literally become my signature on many menus. Therefore, even though it appears in other books of mine, I felt that I simply could not do a book just on desserts without including it.

½ cup fresh fruit puree strained, (or use 2 colors, ¼ cup of each—
mango or papaya and raspberry are most colorful)
1½ cups assorted seasonal fresh fruit sliced in different shapes (melon
balls, wedges of citrus, slivers of peach, whole grapes, etc.)
¼ cup Pastry "Cream" (page 10)

1. Place 2 tablespoons of each color puree on each of two large round plates, preferably white. Spread the puree out in an interesting pattern with the back of a spoon.

2. Arrange ¾ cup of the various fruits in an interesting pattern on the puree, creating a work of art on each plate. Decorate the fruit with the "cream." For a truly exciting treat, use a pastry bag and pipe squiggles, swirls, and rosettes onto the fruit.

MAKES 2 SERVINGS

*Each serving contains approximately: Calories: 154;
Grams of fat: 2.8; Cholesterol: 33 mg; Sodium: 22 mg*

Spiced Poached Pears

These whole spiced pears make a wonderful light dessert for hearty winter meals. I like to serve them with a cookie such as a biscotti. They also work well as an appetizer for some meals.

4 medium-size pears (preferably Bartlett)
¼ cup sugar
4 cinnamon sticks
2 teaspoons allspice berries

1. Place the pears in a saucepan and pour in enough water to cover. Remove the pears. Add the sugar, cinnamon sticks, and allspice to the water and bring to a boil. Reduce the heat to low and simmer for 5 minutes.

2. Peel the pears, leaving the stems attached. Using an apple corer, remove the cores from the ends opposite the stems. Place the peeled, cored pears in the simmering water and continue to simmer until the pears can be easily pierced with a fork, about 8 minutes.

3. Remove from the heat and allow to cool to room temperature. Cover and refrigerate for several hours, or overnight, before serving.

MAKES 4 SERVINGS

*Each serving contains approximately: Calories: 164;
Grams of fat: negligible; Cholesterol: 0; Sodium: 1 mg*

Orange Sections
with Raspberry Vinaigrette

This is a wonderful dessert for a brunch menu when you want something with a little tang that's not too sweet.

3 large, seedless oranges, peeled, sectioned, and membranes removed

FOR THE VINAIGRETTE
1 cup fresh or thawed frozen unsweetened raspberries
½ cup fresh orange juice
2 tablespoons raspberry vinegar
1 tablespoon honey
1 tablespoon extra virgin olive oil
⅛ teaspoon salt

1. Combine all the vinaigrette ingredients in a blender and puree. Press through a fine strainer to remove the seeds. Cover and refrigerate until cold.

2. To serve, divide the orange sections among six plates. Pour ¼ cup of the vinaigrette over each serving.

MAKES 6 SERVINGS

Each serving contains approximately: Calories: 82; Grams of fat: 2.3; Cholesterol: 0; Sodium: 51 mg

Microwave Marvel
with Pastry "Cream"

FOR THE PASTRY "CREAM" (MAKES 1 CUP)
1 cup low-fat ricotta cheese
2 tablespoons sugar or honey
1 teaspoon pure vanilla extract

Cook It Light Desserts

FOR THE "MARVEL"

8 fresh peaches, peeled, pitted, and sliced
2 teaspoons ground cinnamon

1. Combine the cream ingredients in a food processor and blend until satin smooth. Store, covered, in the refigerator.

2. Place the sliced peaches in a nonmetal bowl and add water to a depth of ¼ inch. Sprinkle the cinnamon evenly over the top. Place in a microwave oven and cook on high for 2 minutes. Remove from the oven and spoon the cream over the top. Return to the microwave and cook on high for 1 more minute. Serve warm.

MAKES EIGHT ¾-CUP SERVINGS

Each serving contains approximately: Calories: 99; Grams of fat: 2.5; Cholesterol: 9 mg; Sodium: 39 mg

Wine-Poached Pink Grapefruit

These tasty poached grapefruit are a wonderful last course for a hearty meal. You can either serve them at room temperature or refrigerate and serve cold. I like them best at room temperature accompanied by almond biscotti.

4 small pink grapefruit
1 cup water
2 tablespoons sugar
3 cups dry white wine
½ cup dark raisins
1 teaspoon unflavored gelatin
¼ cup cool water
2 tablespoons Cointreau or other orange-flavored liqueur

1. Using a peeler, remove just the pink part of the grapefruit rind and cut it into matchstick-size strips. Bring the water and sugar to a boil. Add the grapefruit strips and simmer for 5 minutes over low heat. Drain and place the strips in ice water. Set aside.

2. Remove all remaining white pith from the grapefruit and put the fruit into a large saucepan. Add the wine and raisins and bring to a boil. Reduce the heat to low and simmer for 12 minutes, turning frequently. Remove the grapefruit with a slotted spoon and place them on a serving plate or on individual dishes. Set aside.

3. Stir the gelatin into the cool water and allow to soften. Bring the poaching liquid back to a boil and remove from the heat. Add the softened gelatin and stir until the gelatin is completely dissolved. Add the Cointreau and half the grapefruit strips and mix well. Allow to cool to room temperature.

4. To serve, spoon the sauce over the poached grapefruit. Sprinkle the remaining grapefruit strips over the top.

MAKES 4 SERVINGS

Each serving contains approximately: Calories: 303; Grams of fat: negligible; Cholesterol: 0; Sodium: 11 mg

Baked Apples

This is the easiest, best, and healthiest recipe for baked apples imaginable. Golden Delicious apples are so sweet that they don't need sugar; the cinnamon and vanilla enhance their flavor. Serve them warm topped with a dollop of Pastry "Cream" (page 10), vanilla ice milk, or nonfat frozen yogurt.

4 medium-size Golden Delicious apples, cored
2 teaspoons ground cinnamon
1 teaspoon pure vanilla extract

1. Preheat the oven to 350°F. Arrange the cored apples, right side up, in an ovenproof casserole or baking dish just large enough to hold the apples. Add water to a depth of ½ inch. Sprinkle the tops of the apples with the cinnamon and add the extract to the water.

2. Cover with a lid or aluminum foil and bake until the apples can easily be pierced with a fork, about 1 hour.

Each serving contains approximately: Calories: 136;
Grams of fat: negligible; Cholesterol: 0; Sodium: negligible

Baked Papaya

This dessert is particularly nice served as part of an Asian-influenced menu. It is good served plain or with a scoop of vanilla ice milk or nonfat frozen yogurt placed in the center of each warm papaya half.

2 ripe papayas
¼ cup honey
2 teaspoons peeled and finely chopped fresh ginger

1. Preheat the oven to 350°F. Cut the papayas in half lengthwise and remove the seeds. Combine the honey and ginger and mix well. Spread 1 tablespoon of this mixture on each papaya half.

2. Place the papaya halves cut side up in a baking dish sprayed with nonstick vegetable spray and bake until lightly browned, about 30 minutes. Serve warm.

MAKES 4 SERVINGS

Each serving contains approximately: Calories: 100;
Grams of fat: negligible; Cholesterol: 0; Sodium: 5 mg

Broiled Bananas

When you cook bananas, you concentrate their natural sugars and they taste as though they have been sweetened. This is a delightful, sugar-free dessert which is also wonderful served on cooked cereal, such as oatmeal, for breakfast.

2 medium-size bananas
Vanilla ice milk or nonfat frozen yogurt (optional)

1. Preheat the broiler. Peel the bananas and slice them into halves lengthwise. Place the bananas cut side up on a baking sheet sprayed with nonstick vegetable spray and broil until they start to bubble and turn brown.

2. Serve warm by themselves, or top each banana half with a dollop of ice milk or frozen yogurt.

MAKES 4 SERVINGS

Each serving contains approximately: Calories: 58;
Grams of fat: negligible; Cholesterol: 0; Sodium: 1 mg

Gingered Bananas

These bananas are a wonderful dessert for any type of Asian menu. I also like to serve them with cold sliced chicken as a brunch entrée.

2 large, firm bananas
1 tablespoon corn oil margarine
1 tablespoon peeled and finely chopped fresh ginger
1 tablespoon firmly packed dark brown sugar
1 teaspoon fresh lime juice
Vanilla ice milk (optional)

1. Peel the bananas, then cut them in half crosswise and then in half again lengthwise.

2. Melt the margarine in a 10- or 12-inch skillet. Add the ginger and cook over medium heat until the margarine is bubbly. Place the banana quarters in the skillet cut side down and sprinkle with the sugar. Cook until browned, about 2 minutes. Carefully turn the bananas over and cook until the sauce starts to caramelize, another 2 minutes.

3. Remove from the heat and carefully remove the bananas. Add the lime juice to the skillet and mix well. Drizzle the pan drippings over the bananas. Serve the bananas warm, either by themselves or with a scoop of vanilla ice milk.

MAKES 4 SERVINGS

Each serving contains approximately: Calories: 92; Grams of fat: 3.1; Cholesterol: 0; Sodium: 1 mg

Strawberries in Balsamic Vinegar

This recipe and the following one for Strawberries with Black Pepper were developed by Gary Danko, the executive chef of The Dining Room restaurant in The Ritz Carlton Hotel in San Francisco. He created these delightfully different California strawberry desserts for presentation at the International Food Media Conference in Cincinnati in 1993. I have made them many times since I first tasted his and I always find them refreshing.

2 cups fresh strawberries, hulled and halved
2 tablespoons balsamic vinegar
2 tablespoons sugar

1. Combine all the ingredients in a large bowl and toss gently. Cover and refrigerate 1 hour.

2. Serve in stemmed glasses.

MAKES FOUR ½-CUP SERVINGS

Each serving contains approximately: Calories: 51; Grams of fat: negligible; Cholesterol: 0; Sodium: 1 mg

Strawberries with Black Pepper

I have taken a little liberty with Gary Danko's original recipe for this unusual strawberry dessert. His version had heavy cream in the sauce and was served over rich vanilla ice cream. I don't think the sauce needs the cream since it's being served over ice cream, or in this case, over ice milk!

2 cups fresh strawberries, hulled
3 tablespoons sugar
1 tablespoon Grand Marnier or other orange-flavored liqueur
1 tablespoon brandy
½ teaspoon cracked black pepper
2 cups vanilla ice milk or nonfat frozen vanilla yogurt

1. Combine all the ingredients except the ice milk in a large bowl and toss gently. Cover and refrigerate for 1 hour.

2. Serve over the ice milk.

MAKES FOUR 1-CUP SERVINGS

Each serving contains approximately: Calories: 77;
Grams of fat: negligible; Cholesterol: 0; Sodium: 1 mg

Iced Melon
with Honey and Ginger

This is a recipe that I learned how to make in one of Felicia Sorenson's classes when she was teaching for The Great Chefs program at the Robert Mondavi Winery in the Napa Valley a couple of years ago. Felicia is a famous chef who was born in Sri Lanka and is considered an expert on Southeast Asian cooking as well as the traditional dishes of her native country. This dessert is truly unusual and very refreshing.

One 1-pound honeydew melon, peeled, seeded, and cut into
    ½-inch cubes
One 1-pound cantaloupe, peeled, seeded, and cut into ½-inch cubes
1 pound watermelon, peeled, seeded, and cut into ½ inch cubes
3 tablespoons finely chopped preserved ginger (available in the Asian
    section of most supermarkets)
3 tablespoons honey
½ cup dry white wine

Place all the melon in a large mixing bowl, add the remaining
ingredients, and mix well. Cover and refrigerate until well chilled
before serving.

MAKES 8 SERVINGS

Each serving contains approximately: Calories: 88;
Grams of fat: negligible; Cholesterol: 0; Sodium: 13 mg

Minted Pineapple

One 20-ounce can crushed pineapple in natural juice, undrained
¼ teaspoon pure mint extract

Combine the crushed pineapple and extract and refrigerate,
covered, for 1 hour before serving.

MAKES 8 SCANT ⅓-CUP SERVINGS

Each serving contains approximately: Calories: 46;
Grams of fat: negligible; Cholesterol: 0; Sodium: 1 mg

Sherried Grapes

1 pound large purple grapes
1 cup dry sherry

Wash the grapes thoroughly and pat dry. Divide the grapes into 8 small bunches. Cut a crisscross at the bottom of each grape and carefully remove the seeds, keeping the bunches intact. Put the bunches in a large bowl and pour the sherry over them. Cover and refrigerate for several hours before serving, turning the grapes from time to time so they marinate evenly.

MAKES EIGHT ½-CUP SERVINGS

Each serving contains approximately: Calories: 79;
Grams of fat: negligible; Cholesterol: 0; Sodium: 4 mg

Frozen Grapes

Frozen grapes are a wonderful low-calorie dessert which must be eaten slowly—out of necessity!

Ripe grapes

1. Divide the grapes into small bunches and place in the freezer until very hard; this will take several hours.

2. To serve, place the frozen grape bunches in sherbet dishes, small bowls, or plates.

12 large grapes or 20 Thompson seedless grapes contain approximately:
Calories: 1; Grams of fat: negligible; Cholesterol: 0; Sodium: negligible

Golden Apple Brown Betty

This is a recipe of my grandmother's that I revised for my book *Light and Hearty*. It is so easy to make and so delicious that I just couldn't leave it out of this dessert book. The secret is using Golden Delicious apples rather than the pippins or Granny Smiths usually called for in old-fashioned brown Betty recipes. They are so much sweeter that you can cut back on the amount of sugar without missing it.

> 8 medium-size Golden Delicious apples, peeled, cored, and thinly
>   sliced (about 8 cups)
> ¾ cup frozen unsweetened apple juice concentrate, thawed
> ½ cup dark raisins
> ½ cup plus 3 tablespoons whole-wheat flour
> 1 teaspoon ground cinnamon
> ½ cup quick-cooking rolled oats
> 3 tablespoons firmly packed dark brown sugar
> 3 tablespoons corn oil margarine, melted

1. Preheat the oven to 375°F. In a large bowl, combine the apples, concentrate, raisins, 3 tablespoons of the flour, and the cinnamon. Spoon the mixture into an 11 x 7 x 1½-inch baking dish.

2. Combine the oats, the remaining ½ cup of flour, and the brown sugar. Stir in the melted margarine and mix until crumbly. Sprinkle over the apple mixture and bake until golden brown, about 1 hour.

MAKES 10 SERVINGS

Each serving contains approximately: Calories: 218; Grams of fat: 6;
Cholesterol: 0; Sodium: 55 mg

Peach Crisp

2 cups old-fashioned rolled oats (not quick-cooking)
⅓ cup whole-wheat flour
¼ teaspoon salt
1½ teaspoons ground cinnamon
½ cup frozen unsweetened apple juice concentrate, thawed
1½ teaspoons cornstarch
6 large peaches, peeled, pitted, and sliced (6 cups)
¼ cup pure maple syrup
3 tablespoons canola oil

1. Preheat the oven to 350°F. Spread the oats on a baking sheet and place them in the oven for 10 minutes. Remove from the oven and allow to cool. Place half the toasted oats in a food processor or blender and grind until they have the consistency of flour. Combine the ground oats with the whole oats in a mixing bowl. Add the flour, salt, and cinnamon, mix well, and set aside.

2. Combine the concentrate and cornstarch in a saucepan and mix until the cornstarch is completely dissolved. Bring the mixture to a boil over medium heat and stir until thickened, about 2 minutes. Place the peaches in an 8-inch-square baking dish. Pour the thickened juice over the peaches.

3. Add the maple syrup and oil to the oat mixture and stir until well moistened. Spoon the mixture evenly over the peaches. Bake until golden brown, about 45 minutes.

MAKES 8 SERVINGS

Each serving contains approximately: Calories: 254; Grams of fat: 6.7;
Cholesterol: 0; Sodium: 81 mg

Strawberry Napoleons

8 sheets phyllo dough, thawed according to package instructions
3 cups Pastry "Cream" (page 10), at room temperature
3 cups fresh or thawed fresh-frozen strawberries, hulled and sliced
Confectioners' sugar for dusting
Fanned strawberries for garnish (optional)

1. Preheat the oven to 350°F. Spray a baking sheet with non-stick vegetable spray.

2. Spray a sheet of the phyllo dough with nonstick spray, fold in half and spray again, then fold again and spray again. Cut the folded dough in quarters to make four even rectangles. Cut each rectangle in half. Repeat the process with the remaining sheets of phyllo.

3. Place the rectangles on the baking sheet and bake until lightly browned, 3 to 4 minutes. Watch carefully, as they burn easily.

4. For each napoleon, spread three of the rectangles with 1 tablespoon of the sauce each, then 1 tablespoon of the berries each. Stack the three layers, then top with the remaining rectangle. Lightly dust with confectioners' sugar. Repeat until all sixteen napoleons have been assembled.

MAKES 16 NAPOLEONS

Each napoleon contains approximately: Calories: 107; Grams of fat: 1;
Cholesterol: 1 mg; Sodium: 59 mg

Puddings, Custards, and Trifles

....

T his is my own favorite section in the book. The reason is that I think the recipes that fall into this category are the easiest to revise without losing the taste, texture, and appearance of the originals. Also, I think trifles of all types are the most impressive, really easy to make desserts imaginable for large parties and they can also be make ahead of time.

Vanilla Pudding
....

2 cups low-fat milk
2 tablespoons cornstarch
⅓ cup sugar
4 large egg whites, lightly beaten
2 teaspoons canola oil
1½ teaspoons pure vanilla extract

1. Combine the milk and cornstarch in a saucepan and mix until the cornstarch is completely dissolved. Add the sugar, egg whites, and oil and mix well. Place the pan over medium heat and slowly bring to a boil, stirring continuously with a wire whisk until thickened. Remove from the heat and stir in the vanilla. Allow to cool to room temperature.

2. Either spoon the cooled pudding into one serving bowl or spoon ⅓ cup of it into each of six smaller dishes or sherbet glasses.

MAKES SIX ⅓-CUP SERVINGS

Each serving contains approximately: Calories: 120; Grams of fat: 3.1; Cholesterol: 6 mg; Sodium: 77 mg

Chocolate Pudding

One 12-ounce can evaporated skim milk
4½ teaspoons cornstarch
½ cup unsweetened cocoa powder
½ cup sugar
½ teaspoon ground cinnamon
1 teaspoon pure vanilla extract

1. Combine the milk and cornstarch in a heavy saucepan or in the top of a double boiler over simmering water and stir until the cornstarch is completely dissolved. Add the cocoa, sugar, and cinnamon and mix well. Cook over low heat, stirring frequently, until the mixture comes to a boil. Continue to cook, stirring constantly, until thickened, 2 to 3 minutes.

2. Remove from the heat and stir in the vanilla. Allow to cool to room temperature. Serve immediately or store covered in the refrigerator.

MAKES SIX ⅓-CUP SERVINGS

Each serving contains approximately: Calories: 150; Grams of fat: .8; Cholesterol: 3 mg; Sodium: 114 mg

Cook It Light Desserts

Lemon Sponge Pudding

2 large eggs, separated
¾ cup sugar
Juice of 1 large lemon (scant ¼ cup)
1 teaspoon grated lemon rind
1 tablespoon corn oil margarine, melted
¼ cup all-purpose unbleached flour
1 cup nonfat milk

1. Preheat the oven to 350°F. In a large bowl, using a hand-held electric mixer or wire whisk, beat the egg yolks until light. Add the sugar ¼ cup at a time, blending each addition in well, then beating until the yolks are smooth and light in color.

2. Blend in the lemon juice and rind and melted margarine. Add the flour and milk. Beat well to make a smooth batter.

3. Rinse and dry the beaters very well, then beat the egg whites in a medium-size bowl until stiff but not dry peaks form. Fold the beaten whites gently into the batter.

4. Pour the batter into an ungreased 8-inch-square baking dish (or similarly sized dish). Place in a large pan (a roasting pan) and fill this outer pan with boiling water to come up as far as the batter in the dish. Bake until lightly browned, about 45 minutes.

5. Let cool at least 5 minutes. Serve hot or warm, spooned into small bowls.

Variations:

Using the same proportions for the juice and rind, orange or grapefruit pudding is possible, but they're better if you also include a squirt of lemon juice. For a coffee-flavored pudding, substitute a scant ¼ cup strong black coffee fortified, if possible, with a few drops of pure vanilla extract, for the lemon juice and rind.

MAKES SIX ½-CUP SERVINGS

Each serving contains approximately: Calories: 177; Grams of fat: 3.7;
Cholesterol: 72 mg; Sodium: 42 mg

Vanilla Pots de Crème

Classically, this dessert is made with three cups of heavy cream and at least six egg yolks to make six to eight servings. This clearly puts it off limits to anyone trying to cut back on cholesterol and saturated fats. For this reason many of my readers have requested a lighter version of this creamy custard. I have finally come up with a revision that I really like and I'm sure you will too.

You can either serve pots de crème in the little pots made especially for this dessert or in small ramekins or custard cups.

Two 12-ounce cans evaporated skim milk
2 tablespoons sugar
1 tablespoon corn oil margarine
½ cup nonfat liquid egg substitute, beaten until frothy
1½ teaspoons pure vanilla extract

1. Preheat the oven to 325°F. Heat the milk in the top of a double boiler over simmering water. Add the sugar and margarine and stir until the sugar is dissolved and margarine melted. Add the hot milk mixture to the beaten egg substitute, stirring constantly. Add the vanilla and mix well. Pour into 8 small pots or custard cups.

2. Place the filled pots into a pan containing ¾ inch of hot water and place the pan in the oven. Bake until a knife inserted in the center comes out clean, about 25 minutes. Cool to room temperature and then refrigerate until cold before serving. If using pots with covers, place the tops on before refrigerating.

MAKES 8 SERVINGS

Each serving contains approximately: Calories: 116; Grams of fat: 2;
Cholesterol: 4 mg; Sodium: 158 mg

Smooth and Creamy Flan

2 large eggs
4 large egg whites
2½ cups low-fat milk
One 12-ounce can evaporated skim milk
¼ teaspoon salt
⅓ cup sugar
1 teaspoon ground coriander
2 teaspoons pure vanilla extract
1 teaspoon pure maple extract
Ground cinnamon for garnish

1. Preheat the oven to 300°F. Put all of the ingredients except the cinnamon in a blender and blend well.

2. Pour the mixture into a 6-cup baking dish and sprinkle the top generously with cinnamon.

3. Set the baking dish in a shallow pan filled with warm water that comes ¾ inch up the sides of the dish and bake until the flan is set and a knife inserted near the center comes out clean, about 1 hour and 10 minutes.

4. Cool to room temperature, then chill before serving. Sprinkle each serving with cinnamon.

MAKES EIGHT ½-CUP SERVINGS

Each serving contains approximately: Calories: 140; Grams of fat: 2.8; Cholesterol: 61 mg; Sodium: 211 mg

Cappuccino Brûlée

Crème brûlée was actually invented in England where it was called burnt cream. The French adopted it and changed its name. Now I have created an Italian version. If possible, make the custard the day before you plan to serve this dessert just to be certain that it is set before adding the caramel topping.

One 12-ounce can evaporated skim milk
2 tablespoons cornstarch
⅓ cup firmly packed dark brown sugar
4 large egg whites, lightly beaten
2 teaspoons canola oil
2 tablespoons instant coffee granules
½ cup boiling water
1 cinnamon stick, broken in half
1 teaspoon pure vanilla extract
2 tablespoons granulated sugar

1. Combine the milk and cornstarch in a heavy saucepan or in the top of a double boiler over simmering water and stir until the cornstarch is completely dissolved. Add the brown sugar, egg whites, and oil and mix well. Dissolve the instant coffee in the boiling water, then add to the mixture and mix well. Add the cinnamon stick and bring the mixture slowly to a simmer over low heat, stirring frequently. Simmer, stirring constantly, until thickened, about 3 minutes. Remove from the heat and stir in the vanilla. Allow to cool slightly, then spoon ⅓ cup of the mixture into each of 6 ramekins or gratin dishes. Cover with plastic wrap and refrigerate until cold.

2. Uncover the dishes and sprinkle the top of each one with 1 teaspoon of the granulated sugar. Arrange the ramekins on a baking sheet and place them under a preheated broiler until the sugar melts and starts to brown. Serve immediately.

MAKES 6 SERVINGS

Each serving contains approximately: Calories: 124; Grams of fat: 1; Cholesterol: 2 mg; Sodium: 105 mg

Pecan Pudding

This pudding is a lower-calorie, custardlike version of a pecan praline and just as delicious. You can also make this recipe in a pie pan on either a regular or a graham cracker crust and call it Pecan Praline Pie.

2 cups pecan halves (½ pound)
¼ cup water
2 envelopes unflavored gelatin
5 cups nonfat or skim milk
½ cup (1 stick) corn oil margarine
1½ cups firmly packed dark brown sugar
4 teaspoons pure vanilla extract

1. Preheat the oven to 350°F. Coarsely chop 1 cup of the pecans and leave the remaining cup as is. Spread the pecans out (keeping the chopped nuts separate from the halved ones) in a single layer on an ungreased baking sheet and place in the oven until browned, 8 to 10 minutes. Watch carefully as they burn easily. Set aside.

2. Add the water to the gelatin and allow to soften.

3. Combine the milk, margarine, and sugar in a large saucepan and cook over medium heat, stirring constantly with a wire whisk. Just before the mixture comes to a boil, immediately remove from the heat. (If allowed to boil, the mixture will separate and have a grainy texture. This does not ruin the taste, but it does detract from the appearance.) Add the vanilla and gelatin and mix well. Allow to cool to room temperature.

4. Pour ½ cup of the mixture into each of sixteen ramekins or custard cups. Add 1 tablespoon of the toasted chopped pecans to each dish and mix well. (They will rise back to the top.) Arrange 5 pecan halves on the top of each serving for garnish. Refrigerate for at least 4 hours before serving. If you do not have small ramekins, pour the mixture into a large casserole or soufflé dish. Add the

chopped pecans, reserving the whole pecans to garnish the individual servings when they are scooped into serving bowls.

MAKES SIXTEEN ½-CUP SERVINGS

Each serving contains approximately: Calories: 227; Grams of fat: 15.6; Cholesterol: 1 mg; Sodium: 44 mg

Vanilla Yogurt Terrine
with Fruit Coulis

If you really want to impress your family and friends, present them with this gorgeous yogurt terrine for breakfast, brunch, or dessert. It was created by Adam Odegard, the executive chef at The Peninsula Hotel in New York, for the opening of their sensational urban spa. This light and scrumptious dish drew rave reviews from the food writers in attendance at the press breakfast. Now you can either go to New York and order it from their menu or stay home and make it yourself.

> *1 envelope unflavored gelatin*
> *½ cup cold water*
> *1 cup nonfat milk*
> *2 teaspoons grated lemon rind*
> *1 teaspoon pure vanilla extract*
> *2 cups nonfat plain yogurt*
> *1½ cups fruit puree (such as mango or strained raspberry)*
> *6 tablespoons toasted wheat germ*
> *Fresh mint sprigs for garnish (optional)*
> *Melon balls for garnish (optional)*

1. Combine the gelatin and water and allow to stand for 5 minutes.

2. Combine the milk and lemon rind and place in a saucepan over low heat. As soon as it starts to simmer, remove from the heat (watch carefully to make sure the milk doesn't burn). Add the soft-

ened gelatin and stir until the gelatin is completely dissolved. Add the vanilla and yogurt and mix until smooth.

3. Spray six ramekins or decorative molds with nonstick vegetable spray. Pour ½ cup of the yogurt mixture into each. Refrigerate until firm.

4. To serve, "paint" the bottoms of each of six plates with ¼ cup of the fruit puree. Place 1 tablespoon of wheat germ in the center of each plate and unmold the terrines on top of the wheat germ. Garnish with mint sprigs and melon balls if desired.

MAKES 6 SERVINGS

Each serving contains approximately: Calories: 115; Grams of fat: 1; Cholesterol: 2 mg; Sodium: 84 mg

Blueberries Romanoff

When fresh blueberries are not available, you can substitute thawed frozen blueberries. The dessert won't be as pretty, but it will still be very tasty. Also, you can use other berries such as raspberries or strawberries in place of the blueberries, or a combination of all three for a Berry Medley Romanoff.

1 cup nonfat milk
1 tablespoon cornstarch
2 tablespoons sugar
1½ teaspoons pure vanilla extract
2 tablespoons Grand Marnier or other orange-flavored liqueur
2 large egg whites
⅛ teaspoon cream of tartar
4 cups fresh blueberries, picked over and rinsed
Fresh mint sprigs for garnish (optional)

1. Combine the milk, cornstarch, and sugar in a saucepan and stir until the cornstarch is completely dissolved. Place the pan over medium-low heat and slowly bring to a boil. Reduce the heat to

low and simmer, stirring constantly, until thickened. Remove from the heat and cool to room temperature. Add the vanilla and Grand Marnier and mix well.

2. Combine the egg whites and cream of tartar and beat with an electric mixer until stiff but not dry peaks form. Fold the beaten egg whites into the sauce, then fold in the blueberries.

3. Spoon into eight sherbet glasses and garnish each serving with a mint sprig if desired.

MAKES 8 SERVINGS

*Each serving contains approximately: Calories: 81;
Grams of fat: negligible; Cholesterol: 1 mg; Sodium: 38 mg*

Raspberry Fool

A fool is an old-fashioned English dessert. Originally fools were made of pureed cooked fruit that was strained, chilled, and folded into whipped cream. I prefer using the whole fruit and a lighter base than the whipping cream. You may substitute other types of berries, or any chopped fresh fruit, for the raspberries called for in this recipe and adjust the amount of sugar accordingly.

*One 12-ounce can evaporated skim milk
1 tablespoon cornstarch
¼ cup sugar
2 cups fresh raspberries or one 12-ounce package frozen unsweetened
    raspberries, thawed
2 cups nonfat plain yogurt
Fresh raspberries for garnish (optional)*

1. Combine the milk and cornstarch in a heavy saucepan and stir until the cornstarch is completely dissolved. Add the sugar and mix well. Slowly bring to a boil over medium heat, stirring frequently. Reduce the heat to low and simmer, stirring constantly, until thickened, about 5 minutes. Remove from the heat and stir in the raspberries. Allow to cool to room temperature.

2. Fold the yogurt into the cooled mixture and refrigerate, covered, until chilled before serving. To serve spoon ½ cup of the mixture into each of eight small bowls or sherbet glasses.

MAKES EIGHT ½-CUP SERVINGS

Each serving contains approximately: Calories: 110
Grams of fat: negligible; Cholesterol: 3 mg; Sodium: 93 mg

Baked Pineapple Pudding

This is a wonderful light dessert. The last time I served it for dinner, I had the cold leftover pudding for breakfast and it was wonderful then too!

One 15-ounce container low-fat ricotta cheese
⅓ cup firmly packed light brown sugar
2 tablespoons all-purpose unbleached flour
¼ teaspoon ground cinnamon
3 large egg whites
1 tablespoon canola oil
1 teaspoon pure vanilla extract
One 8-ounce can crushed pineapple packed in natural juice, drained

1. Preheat the oven to 400°F. Combine all the ingredients, except the pineapple, in a food processor fitted with the metal blade. Blend just until smooth, about 10 seconds. Add the drained pineapple and blend just until well mixed.

2. Pour the mixture into an 8-inch-square glass baking dish sprayed with nonstick vegetable spray. Bake for 10 minutes. Reduce the oven temperature to 350°F and bake until a knife inserted in the center comes out clean, about 20 more minutes. Serve warm, at room temperature, or refrigerate and serve cold.

MAKES SIX ½-CUP SERVINGS

Each serving contains approximately: Calories: 187; Grams of fat: 7.9;
Cholesterol: 22 mg; Sodium: 118 mg

Pumpkin Pudding

This pudding is a delightful light cold dessert. I also like to serve it hot with holiday meals in place of candied yams.

One 16-ounce can solid pack pumpkin
1½ teaspoons ground cinnamon
¼ teaspoon freshly grated nutmeg
1 teaspoon pure vanilla extract
1 tablespoon canola oil
⅓ cup honey
1 cup nonfat milk, heated to the boiling point
4 large egg whites, lightly beaten

1. Preheat the oven to 350°F. Combine the pumpkin, cinnamon, nutmeg, vanilla, oil, and honey in a large bowl and mix thoroughly. Add the hot milk and egg whites and mix thoroughly.

2. Pour the mixture into a 7 x 11-inch or 8-inch-square baking dish and bake until a knife inserted in the center comes out clean, about 35 minutes. Remove from the oven and cool on a rack. Cover and refrigerate until cold before serving.

MAKES TWELVE ¼-CUP SERVINGS

Each serving contains approximately: Calories: 50; Grams of fat: 1.2; Cholesterol: 0; Sodium: 29 mg

Carrot Pudding

2 tablespoons corn oil margarine
⅔ cup firmly packed dark brown sugar
½ cup unsweetened applesauce
1 large egg plus 2 large egg whites, lightly beaten together
1½ cups whole-wheat flour
1 teaspoon baking soda

2 teaspoons baking powder
½ teaspoon ground mace
1 teaspoon ground cinnamon
2 teaspoons grated orange rind
¼ cup fresh orange juice
½ pound carrots, grated (2 cups)

1. Preheat the oven to 350°F. Combine the margarine and brown sugar in a medium-size bowl and mix until completely blended. Add the applesauce and beaten eggs and mix well.

2. In a large bowl combine the flour, baking soda, baking powder, mace, and cinnamon and mix well. Add the applesauce mixture to the flour mixture and combine until well moistened. Mix in the orange rind and juice and carrots. Spoon the mixture into a 9-inch-square baking pan that has been sprayed with a non-stick vegetable spray and bake until a knife inserted in the center comes out clean, about 1 hour. Cut into 12 pieces.

MAKES 12 SERVINGS

Each serving contains approximately: Calories: 139; Grams of fat: 2.6;
Cholesterol: 18 mg; Sodium: 154 mg

Tapioca Pudding

This is a creamy and delicious version of an old-fashioned favorite. It is good served alone or accompanied by fresh fruit. In the summer I particularly like it with sliced fresh peaches or nectarines.

3 cups nonfat milk
⅓ cup sugar
¼ cup quick-cooking (instant) tapioca
¼ teaspoon salt
¼ cup nonfat liquid egg substitute
1 large egg white
1 teaspoon pure vanilla extract

1. Combine the milk, sugar, tapioca, salt, egg substitute, and egg white in the top of a double boiler and mix well. Cook, over rapidly boiling water, without stirring, for 7 minutes. Continue to cook, stirring constantly, for 6 more minutes. Remove from the heat and stir in the vanilla. Allow to cool to room temperature. The pudding will thicken as it cools.

2. Either serve at room temperature, or cover and refrigerate until cold.

MAKES SIX ½-CUP SERVINGS

Lemon Tapioca:

Substitute 1 teaspoon freshly grated lemon rind for the vanilla extract.

Each serving contains approximately: Calories: 120; Grams of fat: negligible; Cholesterol: 2 mg; Sodium: 189 mg

Creamy Rice Pudding

⅓ cup long-grain white rice (brown rice will not work, nor will instant, quick-cooking, or converted rice)
3 cups low-fat milk
1 tablespoon finely grated lemon rind
⅛ teaspoon salt
¼ cup sugar
1 tablespoon pure vanilla extract

1. Preheat the oven to 325°F. Place the rice in a medium-size saucepan and cover with water by at least 3 inches. Bring to a boil over medium heat and continue to boil for 5 minutes. Drain and rinse the rice. Drain again thoroughly and set aside.

2. While the rice is boiling, pour 1 cup of the milk into another saucepan, add the lemon rind and bring to a boil. Watch it

carefully to avoid scorching or boiling over. As soon as the milk comes to a boil, remove from the heat and add the salt and sugar. Mix until thoroughly dissolved.

3. Pour the hot milk mixture into a 3-quart casserole. Add the vanilla and remaining 2 cups milk. Add the drained rice and mix well. Cover tightly with a lid or aluminum foil and place on top of a baking sheet in the center of the oven. (The baking sheet is to catch the drippings if the pudding boils over during baking.) Bake 2 hours and 45 minutes. Do not uncover during the baking.

MAKES SIX ½-CUP SERVINGS

Each serving contains approximately: Calories: 135; Grams of fat: 2; Cholesterol: 9 mg; Sodium: 112 mg

Basmati Rice Pudding

This exotically seasoned sweet rice is a typically Indian dessert. The only difference between the way it is made in India and this recipe is that they use coconut milk, a highly saturated fat; I have used evaporated skim milk and coconut extract to achieve a very similar taste and texture.

Two 12-ounce cans evaporated skim milk
¼ cup basmati rice
⅛ teaspoon ground cardamom
3 tablespoons sugar
1 teaspoon pure coconut extract

1. Combine 1 can of the milk and the rice in the top of a double boiler over simmering water. Cook over medium heat, stirring frequently, for 20 minutes.

2. Add the remaining can of milk and the cardamom and sugar and mix well. Continue to simmer the mixture, stirring frequently, until it has thickened to a pudding consistency, about 1 hour.

Remove from the heat and stir in the extract. Allow to cool to room temperature, then cover and refrigerate until cold before serving.

MAKES SIX ⅓-CUP SERVINGS

Each serving contains approximately: Calories: 141;
Grams of fat: negligible; Cholesterol: 4 mg; Sodium: 131 mg

Sticky Black Rice Pudding

The original recipe for this unusual dessert called for coconut milk. In order to avoid the saturated fat in the coconut milk, I used non-fat milk and coconut extract which works amazingly well. I also added the mango puree which I think enhances the taste and appearance of this dramatic dessert. You will probably have to go to an Asian market to find the sticky, or sweet, black rice, but it is well worth the trip!

> 1 cup sticky (sweet) black rice
> 4 cups water
> ¼ cup nonfat milk
> 3 large egg whites, lightly beaten
> 3 tablespoons sugar
> 1 tablespoon pure coconut extract
> One 8-ounce can water chestnuts, drained and diced (½ cup)
> One 8-ounce can crushed pineapple packed in natural juice, drained
>   (⅔ cup)
> 2 pounds fresh mangoes, peeled, pitted, and pureed (2 cups)

1. Combine the rice and water in a heavy saucepan and bring to a boil over medium-high heat. Continue to boil until the surface water has evaporated and there are "craters" on the top. Reduce the heat as low as possible and continue to simmer, covered, for 20 minutes. Uncover and allow to cool to room temperature.

2. Preheat the oven to 325°F. Combine the cooked rice with the remaining ingredients (except the mango puree) and mix well. Spoon the rice mixture into a baking dish or casserole and bake

until all the liquid is absorbed, about 45 minutes. Remove from the oven and allow to cool to room temperature. Cover and refrigerate until cold before serving.

3. To serve, strain the mango puree to remove any lumps and pour ¼ cup of it over each of eight plates. Tilt each plate, rotating it until the puree covers its surface. Press ⅓ cup of the rice pudding into a mold and then unmold it onto the blade of a spatula. Carefully place the pudding in the center of the mango-covered plate and serve.

MAKES EIGHT ⅓-CUP SERVINGS

Each serving contains approximately: Calories: 447;
Grams of fat: negligible; Cholesterol: 4 mg; Sodium: 170 mg

Rum-Raisin Risotto

I have always loved the texture of risotto. A few months ago I started working on the concept of dessert risottos, replacing the usual stock and wine called for with fruit juices and milk. To date this rum-raisin Risotto is my favorite creation. I served it recently for a dinner party and all of my guests wanted the recipe—which is always a good sign!

3 tablespoons corn oil margarine
1 large Golden Delicious apple, peeled, cored, and finely diced
(1½ cups)
¾ cup arborio rice
⅓ cup dark raisins
¼ cup dark rum
1 cup unsweetened apple juice
2 tablespoons firmly packed dark brown sugar
One 12-ounce can evaporated skim milk
1½ cups nonfat milk

1. Melt 2 tablespoons of the margarine in a large, heavy saucepan over medium heat. Add the apples and cook, stirring

frequently, until tender. Add the rice, raisins, and rum and cook, stirring constantly, until all of the rum is absorbed. Add ½ cup of the apple juice and cook, stirring, until almost dry. Add the remaining apple juice and again reduce, stirring, until almost dry. Add the sugar and mix well.

2. Combine the milks and start adding it ½ cup at a time to the rice mixture, always stirring frequently and allowing almost all of it to be absorbed before adding more. Do not allow the last addition of milk to be completely absorbed; risotto should have a creamy, cereallike consistency. Remove from the heat and stir in the remaining 1 tablespoon of margarine. Serve warm.

MAKES TEN ½-CUP SERVINGS

Each serving contains approximately: Calories: 187; Grams of fat: 3.8; Cholesterol: 2 mg; Sodium: 61 mg

Tropical Trifle

I adore trifles for parties. They are so easy to make and they can be made well ahead of time. For this reason I have been trying all kinds of different fruit and flavor combinations lately and this rather exotic, Caribbean variation is sure to both please and surprise your guests.

> 2 cups nonfat milk
> 2 tablespoons cornstarch
> ⅓ cup sugar
> 4 large egg whites, lightly beaten
> 2 teaspoons canola oil
> 1½ teaspoons pure vanilla extract
> 1 teaspoon pure coconut extract
> One 8-ounce angel food cake, cut into 1-inch cubes (4 cups)
> ¼ cup dark rum
> One 20-ounce can pineapple chunks packed in natural juice, drained
>   (2 cups)
> 3 large mangoes, peeled, pitted, and diced (3 cups)

1. Combine the milk and cornstarch in a saucepan and mix until the cornstarch is completely dissolved. Add the sugar, egg whites, and oil and mix well. Slowly bring to a boil over medium-low heat, stirring constantly with a wire whisk until thickened. Remove from the heat, add the extracts, mix well, and allow to come to room temperature.

2. To assemble the trifle, place one third of the cake pieces in the bottom of a 2-quart glass bowl or trifle dish. Sprinkle with one third of the rum. Spoon ⅔ cup of the custard evenly over the cake. Spoon one third of the pineapple chunks and one third of the diced mangoes over the custard. Repeat the process twice.

3. Serve immediately or cover and refrigerate.

MAKES TWELVE ⅔-CUP SERVINGS

*Each serving contains approximately: Calories: 184; Grams of fat: 1.1;
Cholesterol: 1 mg; Sodium: 94 mg*

Cherry Trifle

Whenever you serve this scrumptious dessert, everyone will be surprised to learn how low in calories it is and that it contains practically no cholesterol.

2 cups nonfat milk
2 tablespoons cornstarch
⅓ cup sugar
4 large egg whites, lightly beaten
2 teaspoons canola oil
1½ teaspoons pure vanilla extract
6 tablespoons dry sherry
One 8-ounce angel food cake, cut into 1-inch cubes (4 cups)
*Two 16-ounce packages frozen unsweetened pitted dark cherries,
    thawed (4 cups)*

1. Combine the milk and cornstarch in a saucepan and mix until the cornstarch is completely dissolved. Add the sugar, egg whites, and oil and mix well. Slowly bring to a boil over medium-low heat, stirring constantly with a wire whisk until thickened. Remove from the heat and add the vanilla and 3 tablespoons of the sherry. Mix well and allow to cool to room temperature.

2. To assemble the trifle, place one third of the cake pieces in the bottom of a 2-quart glass bowl or trifle dish. Sprinkle with 1 tablespoon of the remaining sherry, then spoon ⅔ cup of the custard evenly over the cake. Spoon 1⅓ cups of the cherries over the custard. Repeat this process two more times. Serve immediately, or cover and refrigerate until cold.

MAKES TWELVE ¾-CUP SERVINGS

Each serving contains approximately: Calories: 158; Grams of fat: 1; Cholesterol: 1 mg; Sodium: 96 mg

Peach Melba Trifle

This classic combination of peaches and raspberries is best in the summertime when you can get really glorious fresh and flavorful fruit. However, I have made this dessert in the dead of winter using frozen peaches and raspberries and it is still a delicious and impressive dessert.

2 cups nonfat milk
2 tablespoons cornstarch
⅓ cup sugar
4 large egg whites, lightly beaten
2 teaspoons canola oil
1½ teaspoons pure vanilla extract
6 tablespoons Grand Marnier or other orange-flavored liqueur
One 8-ounce angel food cake, cut into 1-inch cubes (4 cups)
3 large, ripe peaches, peeled, pitted, and sliced (4 cups)
2 cups fresh raspberries

1. Combine the milk and cornstarch in a saucepan and mix until the cornstarch is completely dissolved. Add the sugar, egg whites, and oil and mix well. Slowly bring to a boil over medium-low heat, stirring constantly with a wire whisk until thickened. Remove from the heat and allow to come to room temperature. When cooled, add the vanilla and 2 tablespoons of the Grand Marnier.

2. To assemble the trifle, place one third of the cake pieces in the bottom of a 2-quart glass bowl or trifle dish. Sprinkle with 4 teaspoons of the remaining Grand Marnier. Spoon ⅔ cup of the custard over the cake. Spoon one third of the peaches and one third of the raspberries over the custard. Repeat the process twice.

3. Serve immediately or cover and refrigerate.

MAKES TWELVE ¾-CUP SERVINGS

Each serving contains approximately: Calories: 136; Grams of fat: 1; Cholesterol: 1 mg; Sodium: 93 mg

Lemon Angel

This sensational lemon dessert is a revision of a recipe that a friend of mine frequently serves for dinner parties. I asked her for the recipe because my husband absolutely loved it. When I saw the ingredients I immediately started working on a lighter version that I could pass on to my readers. The good news is that my friend now uses my recipe for her parties! It is a perfect dessert for entertaining because it must be made ahead of time and refrigerated for several hours, or overnight, before serving.

3 tablespoons corn oil margarine
1 cup sugar
¾ cup fresh lemon juice
1 tablespoon grated lemon rind
2 large eggs
6 large egg whites
One 8-ounce angel food cake, thinly sliced

1. Combine the margarine and sugar in the top of a double boiler over simmering water. Cook over medium-high heat until the margarine is melted. Add the lemon juice and rind and mix well.

2. Combine the eggs and egg whites in a medium-size bowl and beat until frothy. Add them to the mixture in the double boiler and cook, stirring constantly, until thick, about 10 minutes. Remove from the heat and allow to cool slightly.

3. Place one third of the cake slices in the bottom of a soufflé dish. Cover with 1 cup of the lemon sauce. Repeat the layering two more times, ending with a layer of lemon sauce on the top. Cover tightly and refrigerate for at least 6 hours or overnight before serving.

MAKES EIGHT ¾-CUP SERVINGS

Each serving contains approximately: Calories: 250; Grams of fat: 6; Cholesterol: 53 mg; Sodium: 185 mg

Bread Pudding with Whiskey Sauce

This old-fashioned, Southern bread pudding is the ultimate in "comfort food." If you prefer not to use whiskey in the sauce, you can flavor the melted ice milk with an extract such as vanilla, brandy, or rum.

2 cups nonfat milk
½ cup sugar
½ teaspoon ground cinnamon
⅛ teaspoon salt
3 tablespoons corn oil margarine
4 large egg whites, lightly beaten
3 cups cubed and lightly toasted bread

1 large Golden Delicious apple, peeled, cored, and finely diced
  (1½ cups)
½ cup dark raisins

FOR THE WHISKEY SAUCE
1 cup vanilla ice milk, melted
2 tablespoons whiskey

1. Preheat the oven to 350°F. Pour the milk in a saucepan and bring almost to the boiling point; do not allow it to come to a boil. Remove from the heat and add the sugar, cinnamon, salt, and margarine. Stir until the margarine is completely melted.

2. Pour the mixture into a large bowl with the egg whites and mix thoroughly. Fold in the toasted bread cubes, apple, and raisins. Spoon into a 1½-quart baking dish sprayed with a nonstick vegetable spray. Bake until a knife inserted in the center comes out clean, about 45 minutes.

3. While the pudding is baking, make the sauce by combining the ice milk and whiskey until smooth.

4. Serve the pudding warm with 2 tablespoons of the whiskey sauce poured over each serving.

MAKES EIGHT ½-CUP SERVINGS

Each serving contains approximately: Calories: 320; Grams of fat: 5.4; Cholesterol: 1 mg; Sodium: 397 mg

British Baked Bread Pudding

This is a wonderful way to use bread that is several days old and, as the English say, "past the peak." The pudding is actually more like a cake in texture and I like it best baked in a square cake pan, cut into squares, and served cold.

6 slices "past the peak" whole-wheat bread, crusts removed
1¼ cups nonfat milk
2 large egg whites, lightly beaten
⅓ cup firmly packed dark brown sugar
½ teaspoon ground cinnamon
½ teaspoon ground ginger
¼ teaspoon ground allspice
⅛ teaspoon ground cloves
2 tablespoons corn oil margarine, melted
½ cup dark raisins
Freshly grated nutmeg for garnish

1. Preheat the oven to 350°F. In a large bowl break the bread into crumbs. Pour the milk over the bread and allow to stand until the bread has absorbed the milk, about 30 minutes.

2. In another bowl combine the egg whites with the sugar, cinnamon, ginger, allspice, and cloves and mix until smooth. Stir in the melted margarine, then pour over the milk-soaked bread. Mix, using a pastry blender or a fork, until no lumps remain. Add the raisins and mix well. Spoon the mixture into an 8-inch-square pan that has been sprayed with a nonstick vegetable spray and spread it out evenly. Sprinkle the top of the mixture with nutmeg. Bake until a knife inserted in the center comes out clean, about 1¼ hours. Cut the pudding into 9 squares. This pudding may be served hot or cold. If serving it cold, it is best to wait and cut it after cooling it because it cuts more cleanly.

MAKES 9 SERVINGS

Each serving contains approximately: Calories: 132; Grams of fat: 3.1;
Cholesterol: 1 mg; Sodium: 131 mg

Cook It Light Desserts

Pineapple Bread Pudding

The combination of pineapple and pecans gives this bread pudding a delightfully different taste and texture. It is good served with baked ham or as a dessert.

¼ cup (½ stick) corn oil margarine
¾ cup sugar
½ cup nonfat liquid egg substitute
1 cup buttermilk
One 20-ounce can crushed pineapple packed in natural juice,
*   undrained*
Twelve slices dry white bread, crusts removed and cut into ½-inch
*   cubes (4 cups)*
¼ cup chopped pecans

1. Preheat the oven to 350°F. Spray a 9 x 13-inch baking dish with a nonstick vegetable spray. In a large bowl cream the margarine with ½ cup of the sugar. Beat in the egg substitute and the remaining sugar, mixing thoroughly. Slowly beat in the buttermilk. Add the crushed pineapple and all of the juice from the can and mix well. Fold in the cubed bread.

2. Pour the mixture into the dish and bake until golden brown, about 50 minutes. During the last 8 minutes of baking time, place the chopped pecans, on a baking sheet, in the oven with the pudding to toast them. Watch them carefully, as they burn easily.

3. Sprinkle each serving with 1 teaspoon of the toasted pecans.

MAKES 12 SCANT ½-CUP SERVINGS

Each serving contains approximately: Calories: 238; Grams of fat: 7.2;
Cholesterol: 2 mg; Sodium: 204 mg

Tiramisù

Tiramisù is one of those phenomenal desserts that went from obscurity to prominence practically overnight. Very few people had ever heard of it and the next week you couldn't find a menu without it! There are also many different version of this fabulous Italian concoction, but this is certainly among the lightest.

One 8.8-ounce package mascarpone cheese (1 cup)
1 cup nonfat ricotta cheese
¼ cup sugar
½ cup Amaretto di Saronno or other almond-flavored liqueur
Two 3-ounce packages ladyfingers, top and bottom halves separated
1 cup strong coffee, cooled
2 tablespoons unsweetened cocoa powder

1. In a blender, place the mascarpone, ricotta, sugar, and ¼ cup of the amaretto. Blend on high speed several minutes until the mixture is completely smooth. Set aside.

2. Line an 8-inch springform pan with plastic wrap so liquid will not leak out. Make a layer of ladyfinger halves, fitting them tightly into the bottom of the pan and using up one whole package.

3. Combine the coffee and remaining ¼ cup amaretto. Pour half the liquid evenly over the layer of ladyfingers. Cover with half the cheese mixture. Use the remaining ladyfingers to cover the cheese in a tight layer. Pour the remaining liquid over the ladyfingers and cover with the remaining cheese.

4. Sift the cocoa powder to cover the tiramisù completely. Refrigerate for 6 to 8 hours or overnight before serving. To serve, release and remove the sides of the springform pan, being careful not to damage the tiramisù. Cut into 12 pie-shaped wedges.

MAKES 12 SERVINGS

Each serving contains approximately: Calories: 179; Grams of fat: 8.6; Cholesterol: 75 mg; Sodium: 82 mg

Chocolate Steamed Pudding
with Good-as-Gold Sauce

2 large egg whites
½ cup sugar
3 tablespoons corn oil margarine, melted
1 cup all-purpose unbleached flour
1½ teaspoons baking powder
½ teaspoon baking soda
6 tablespoons unsweetened cocoa powder
⅔ cup nonfat milk

2 tablespoons corn oil margarine, at room temperature
¾ cup confectioners' sugar, sifted
¼ cup nonfat liquid egg substitute
⅓ cup canned evaporated skim milk
1 teaspoon unflavored gelatin
1 tablespoon cool water
2 tablespoons boiling water
½ teaspoon pure vanilla extract

1. For the pudding, in a large bowl beat the egg whites lightly. Gradually beat in the sugar and melted margarine. Combine the flour, baking powder, baking soda, and cocoa in another bowl and add alternately with the milk to the egg white mixture.

2. Pour the batter into the top of a double boiler sprayed with nonstick vegetable coating. Place over simmering water, cover, and cook or steam for 1 ½ hours. Do not lift the cover while steaming.

3. For the sauce, place the margarine in a medium-size bowl and slowly stir in the confectioners' sugar. Slowly stir in the egg substitute and set aside.

4. Pour the milk into another medium-size bowl. Place the bowl in the freezer until the edges start to freeze, about 15 minutes. Meanwhile, soften the gelatin in the cool water. Add the boiling

water and stir until the gelatin is completely dissolved, then set aside. Beat the chilled milk until very thick. Stir in the vanilla, gradually add the gelatin mixture, beating with a whisk or electric mixer until soft peaks form, then fold into the sugar mixture.

5. To serve, invert the warm pudding onto a plate and cut into 6 pie-shaped wedges. Serve immediately topped with the sauce.

MAKES 6 SERVINGS

Each serving contains approximately: Calories: 335; Grams of fat: 16; Cholesterol: 166 mg; Sodium: 331 mg

Year Around Summer Pudding

Summer pudding is a typically English dessert that is usually made with fresh raspberries and fresh red and black currants. Since it is often difficult to find these, I have used raspberries and strawberries instead. I have also called for frozen berries which are available all year around. Of course, in the summer you can certainly use fresh berries rather than frozen.

One 12-ounce package frozen unsweetened raspberries, thawed, or 12 ounces fresh
One 16-ounce package frozen unsweetened strawberries, thawed, or 1 pound fresh
½ cup sugar
8 slices white bread
Fresh raspberries for garnish (optional)

1. Combine the raspberries, strawberries, and sugar in a large, heavy saucepan and bring to a boil over medium heat. Reduce the heat to low and simmer just until the sugar is completely dissolved, about 3 minutes. Remove from the heat and set aside.

2. Spray a 1-quart round-bottomed bowl with nonstick vegetable spray. Line the bowl with 7 slices of the bread, overlapping them and pressing the seams together.

3. Remove ⅔ cup of the liquid from the berry mixture to a small container. Cover and refrigerate. Spoon the berries and remaining juice into the bread-lined bowl. Place the remaining slice of bread on top. Place a small plate on top of the bread and weight it down with a 3-pound weight. (I use two large cans of tomatoes.) Place the weighted pudding in the refrigerator overnight.

4. To serve, turn the pudding over onto a serving plate and remove the bowl. Pour the reserved liquid over the pudding, being careful to cover any of the bread that may still be white. Cut into 6 pie-shaped wedges and garnish each serving with a few fresh raspberries if desired.

MAKES 8 SERVINGS

Each serving contains approximately: Calories: 182; Grams of fat: .98; Cholesterol: .75 mg; Sodium: 117 mg

Passover Pudding

This light and delicately flavored Passover dessert is good served hot or cold. If serving it hot, spoon it out like a pudding and serve it in bowls. If chilled, cut into six pieces and serve on plates.

1 teaspoon grated lemon rind
1½ teaspoons fresh lemon juice
2 medium-size Golden Delicious apples, peeled, cored, and shredded
4 large egg whites (place 2 in each of 2 bowls)
⅛ teaspoon salt
½ cup frozen unsweetened apple juice concentrate, partially thawed
2 teaspoons nonfat dry milk
½ teaspoon ground cinnamon
2 teaspoons canola oil
¼ cup matzo meal
⅓ cup dark raisins, rinsed and drained

1. Preheat the oven to 350°F. Add the lemon rind and juice to the apples, mix well, and set aside.

2. Beat 2 of the egg whites with an electric mixer in a medium-size bowl until frothy. Add the salt and continue beating until stiff but not dry peaks form. Slowly add the apple juice concentrate and continue beating until soft peaks form.

3. Combine the other 2 egg whites with the dry milk, cinnamon, and oil and beat with the same beater until well-mixed. Then fold in the apple juice mixture.

4. Fold in the matzo meal, raisins, and apples. Turn into an 8-inch-square shallow baking dish sprayed with nonstick vegetable spray. Bake until lightly browned on top, 30 to 35 minutes. Serve warm, at room temperature, or cover and refrigerate until cold.

MAKES SIX ½-CUP SERVINGS

Each serving contains approximately: Calories: 135; Grams of fat: 2; Cholesterol: negligible; Sodium: 90 mg

NOTE: Recipe may be doubled to make 12 servings. Bake in a greased 9 x 13-inch baking dish.

Mousses and Soufflés

....

Cold soufflés have always been among my favorite desserts for dinner parties because they are dramatic looking, delicious, and so easy to make. However, since they all contain stiffly beaten raw egg whites, which we are now cautioned not to use, I started trying to achieve the same taste and texture without them. In this section, I have turned all my favorite cold soufflés into mousses, using only very cold, whipped, canned evaporated skim milk and I like the texture even better.

I also find that cooking with evaporated skim milk is a better substitute for the cream called for in most hot soufflé recipes than regular nonfat milk. After tasting my Grand Marnier soufflé, no one is ever going to ask you, "Where's the cream?"

Spiced Apple Mousse

The idea for this mousse started with making a quick and easy apple butter from a jar of unsweetened applesauce. I liked the applesauce apple butter so much on dry cereal with milk or yogurt that I decided it would make a fabulous mousse—and it does!

One 12-ounce can evaporated skim milk, very cold
2 envelopes unflavored gelatin
¼ cup cool water
¼ cup boiling water
2 cups Applesauce Apple Butter (recipe follows)

1. Several hours before you plan to make the mousse, place the can of milk in the refrigerator. Place a large glass, enamel, or stainless-steel mixing bowl and the beaters to an electric mixer in the freezer.

2. Before starting the mousse, if you are going to be using a collared soufflé dish, it is necessary to collar a 1-quart (6-inch diamter) soufflé dish with a waxed paper collar. To collar a soufflé dish, cut a 24-inch length of waxed paper and fold it in half lengthwise, then wrap it around the dish so that it forms a 4-inch-high collar. Secure the collar in place using masking tape, and set aside.

3. Soften the gelatin in the cool water. Add the boiling water and stir until the gelatin is completely dissolved. Allow to cool.

4. Combine the dissolved gelatin and apple butter in a blender and blend until completely smooth. Place the blender container in the refrigerator while you whip the milk.

5. Remove the bowl and beaters from the freezer. Pour the cold milk into the bowl and beat until soft peaks form. Remove the blender from the refrigerator and pour the apple butter mixture into the beaten milk. Using a rubber spatula, fold the mixture into the milk until no streaks of white show. Pour the mixture into the collared soufflé dish, a Bundt pan, or a decorative mold and refrigerate at least 4 hours before uncollaring or unmolding. To serve, carefully

remove the waxed paper collar from the soufflé dish. Cut the top layer, above the dish, into 6 pie-shaped wedges, placing each wedge on a plate. Cut the mousse remaining in the dish into 6 more wedges and place on plates. If using a mold or Bundt pan, briefly dip the bottom of it into hot water and then quickly invert it onto a serving plate, or place the mold or pan upside down on the serving plate and blow hot air on it, using a hair dryer, until the mousse releases from the mold. I prefer the hair-dryer method as the mousse unmolds more perfectly. Then cut the mousse into 12 pie-shaped wedges.

MAKES TWELVE ¾-CUP SERVINGS

Each serving contains approximately: Calories: 69;
Grams of fat: negligible; Cholesterol: 1 mg; Sodium: 38 mg

Applesauce Apple Butter

One 23-ounce jar natural unsweetened applesauce
½ cup frozen unsweetened apple juice concentrate
1¼ teaspoons ground cinnamon
½ teaspoon ground allspice
⅛ teaspoon ground cloves

1. Combine all the ingredients in a blender and blend until smooth.

2. Pour the pureed mixture in a heavy saucepan and bring to a boil over medium heat. Reduce the heat to low and simmer, covered, with the lid ajar to allow the steam to escape, for 20 minutes. Allow to cool to room temperature and store, covered, in the refrigerator, for up to 2 weeks.

MAKES 2½ CUPS

1 tablespoon contains approximately: Calories: 13;
Grams of fat: negligible; Cholesterol: 0; Sodium: 1 mg

Strawberry Mousse
with Raspberry Sauce

FOR THE MOUSSE

One 12-ounce can evaporated skim milk, very cold
2 envelopes unflavored gelatin
¼ cup cool water
¼ cup boiling water
One 16-ounce package frozen unsweetened strawberries, thawed
2 tablespoons fresh lemon juice
3 tablespoons Cointreau or other orange-flavored liqueur
⅓ cup sugar

FOR THE SAUCE (MAKES 1½ CUPS)

One 12-ounce package frozen unsweetened raspberries, completely
    thawed
¼ cup sugar
1 tablespoon fresh lemon juice
1 tablespoon Cointreau or other orange-flavored liqueur

1. Several hours before you plan to make the mousse, put the can of milk in the refrigerator. Place a large stainless-steel, glass, or ceramic bowl and the beaters to an electric mixer in the freezer.

2. Soften the gelatin in the cool water. Add the boiling water and stir until the gelatin is completely dissolved.

3. Place the thawed strawberries in a blender and add the dissolved gelatin, lemon juice, and liqueur and puree. Refrigerate the pureed mixture while you whip the milk.

4. Remove the bowl and beaters from the freezer. Pour the cold milk into the bowl and beat until soft peaks form. Slowly add the sugar and continue beating until firm peaks form. Pour the pureed strawberry mixture into the whipped milk and, using a rubber spatula, carefully fold the puree into the milk until no streaks of white show. Pour the mixture into a 1-quart collared soufflé dish (see page 54 for instructions on how to do this) or a Bundt pan or

mold sprayed with nonstick vegetable spray and refrigerate until firm, at least 4 hours.

5. To make the sauce, combine the sauce ingredients in a blender and puree. Pour through a fine strainer to remove the seeds. Cover and refrigerate until ready to serve.

6. See page 55 for uncollaring and unmolding instructions. Drizzle each serving with 2 tablespoons of the sauce. If you have any leftover mousse, either refrigerate it or freeze to serve as a frozen dessert.

MAKES TWELVE ¾-CUP SERVINGS

Blueberry Mousse:

Substitute completely thawed frozen blueberries for the strawberries called for in step 3.

Each serving contains approximately: Calories: 114;
Grams of fat: negligible; Cholesterol: 1 mg; Sodium: 40 mg

Prune Mousse

This is just as good for breakfast as it is for dessert.

18 dried pitted prunes
1 cup boiling water
1 envelope unflavored gelatin
2 tablespoons cool water
¾ cup low-fat cottage cheese
¾ cup nonfat milk
1 teaspoon pure vanilla extract
¼ teaspoon ground cinnamon

1. Put the pitted prunes in a large bowl and pour ¾ cup of the boiling water over them. Cover and refrigerate for 24 hours. Place the prunes and their soaking water in a blender.

2. Soften the gelatin in the cool water for 5 minutes. Add the remaining ¼ cup boiling water and stir until the gelatin is completely dissolved. Add the gelatin mixture and the remaining ingredients to the blender. Blend on high speed until frothy. Pour into a shallow rectangular or square dish. Cover tightly and refrigerate until firm.

3. To serve, cut into squares and put on plates or in sherbet glasses.

MAKES SIX ¾-CUP SERVINGS

Each serving contains approximately: Calories: 101;
Grams of fat: negligible; Cholesterol: 2 mg; Sodium: 133 mg

Peach Mousse

This is a very delicate mousse both in texture and flavor. It is excellent after a hearty meal garnished with sliced fresh peaches. I usually make it in a Bundt pan and then unmold it onto a serving dish and fill the center with sliced fresh peaches when they are in season or thawed frozen peaches when they aren't.

> One 12-ounce can evaporated skim milk, very cold
> 2 envelopes unflavored gelatin
> ¼ cup cool water
> ¼ cup boiling water
> 3 cups sliced fresh peaches or one 16-ounce package frozen
>   unsweetened sliced peaches, thawed
> ¼ cup sugar
> 1½ teaspoons ground cinnamon
> 2 teaspoons pure vanilla extract

1. Several hours before you plan to make the mousse, place the can of milk in the refrigerator. Place a large stainless-steel, glass, or ceramic bowl and the beaters to an electric mixer in the freezer.

2. Soften the gelatin in the cool water for 5 minutes. Add the boiling water and stir until the gelatin is completely dissolved. Place

the peaches in a blender. Add the sugar, cinnamon, vanilla, and dissolved gelatin mixture and puree. Pour the pureed peach mixture into a bowl and place it in the refrigerator while you whip the milk.

3. Remove the bowl and beaters from the freezer. Pour the cold milk in the bowl and beat until soft peaks form. Remove the peach mixture from the refrigerator (it should have a syrupy consistency) and, using a rubber spatula, carefully fold the puree into the whipped milk until no streaks of white show. Pour the mixture into either a collared 1-quart soufflé dish (see page 54 for instructions for doing this), a Bundt pan, or some other decorative mold or container. Refrigerate for at least 4 hours before serving. See page 55 for instructions on uncollaring and unmolding.

MAKES TWELVE ¾-CUP SERVINGS

Each serving contains approximately: Calories: 63; Grams of fat: negligible; Cholesterol: 1 mg; Sodium: 34 mg

Concord Grape Mousse

I like to make this mousse in a collared soufflé dish and then surround the dish with small bunches of grapes when serving it.

One 12-ounce can evaporated skim milk, very cold
One 12-ounce can frozen unsweetened Concord grape juice concentrate
2 envelopes unflavored gelatin
¼ cup cool water
¼ cup boiling water

1. Several hours before you plan to make the mousse, place the can of milk in the refrigerator. Place a large stainless-steel, glass, or ceramic bowl and the beaters to an electric mixer in the freezer. Place the can of frozen grape juice in the refrigerator to thaw, but remain cold.

2. Soften the gelatin in the cool water for 5 minutes. Add the boiling water and stir until the gelatin is completely dissolved.

Combine the cold thawed grape juice and dissolved gelatin mixture in a small bowl and mix well. Place the bowl in the refrigerator while you whip the milk.

3. Remove the bowl and beaters from the freezer. Pour the cold milk in the bowl and beat until soft peaks form. Remove the grape juice mixture from the refrigerator (it should have a syrupy consistency) and, using a rubber spatula, carefully fold it into the whipped milk until no streaks of white show. Pour the mixture into either a collared 1-quart soufflé dish (see page 54 for instructions on doing this), a Bundt pan, or some other decorative mold or container. Refrigerate for at least 4 hours before serving. See page 55 for instructions on uncollaring and unmolding.

MAKES TWELVE ¾-CUP SERVINGS

Each serving contains approximately: Calories: 78;
Grams of fat: negligible; Cholesterol: 1 mg; Sodium: 36 mg

Orange Mousse

One 12-ounce can evaporated skim milk, very cold
One 12-ounce can frozen unsweetened orange juice concentrate
2 envelopes unflavored gelatin
¼ cup cool water
¼ cup boiling water
⅓ cup sugar
1 teaspoon pure vanilla extract
3 tablespoons Grand Marnier or other orange-flavored liqueur

1. Several hours before you plan to make the mousse, place the can of milk in the refrigerator. Place a large stainless-steel, glass, or ceramic bowl and the beaters to an electric mixer in the freezer. Place the can of frozen orange juice in the refrigerator to thaw, but remain cold.

2. Soften the gelatin in the cool water for 5 minutes. Add the boiling water and stir until the gelatin is completely dissolved.

Combine the cold thawed orange juice, sugar, vanilla, Grand Marnier, and dissolved gelatin mixture in a small bowl and mix well. Place the bowl in the refrigerator while you whip the milk.

3. Remove the bowl and beaters from the freezer. Pour the cold milk in the bowl and beat until soft peaks form. Remove the orange juice mixture from the refrigerator (it should have a syrupy consistency) and, using a rubber spatula, carefully fold it into the whipped milk until no streaks of white show. Pour the mixture into either a collared 1-quart soufflé dish (see page 54 for instructions on doing this), a Bundt pan, or some other decorative mold or container. Refrigerate for at least 4 hours before serving. See page 55 for instructions on uncollaring and unmolding.

MAKES TWELVE ¾-CUP SERVINGS

Grapefruit Mousse:

Substitute one 12-ounce can frozen unsweetened grapefruit juice concentrate for the orange juice concentrate.

*Each serving contains approximately: Calories: 65;
Grams of fat: negligible; Cholesterol: 1 mg; Sodium: 34 mg*

Lemon Mousse

*One 12-ounce can evaporated skim milk, very cold
One 12-ounce can frozen lemonade concentrate
2 envelopes unflavored gelatin
¼ cup cool water
¼ cup boiling water
1 teaspoon finely grated lemon rind*

1. Several hours before you plan to make the mousse, place the can of milk in the refrigerator. Place a large stainless-steel, glass, or ceramic bowl and the beaters to an electric mixer in the freezer. Place the can of frozen lemonade in the refrigerator to thaw, but remain cold.

2. Soften the gelatin in the cool water for 5 minutes. Add the boiling water and stir until the gelatin is completely dissolved. Combine the cold thawed lemonade, grated lemon rind, and dissolved gelatin mixture in a small bowl and mix well. Place the bowl in the refrigerator while you whip the milk.

3. Remove the bowl and beaters from the freezer. Pour the cold milk in the bowl and beat until soft peaks form. Remove the lemonade mixture from the refrigerator (it should have a syrupy consistency) and, using a rubber spatula, carefully fold it into the whipped milk until no streaks of white show. Pour the mixture into either a collared 1-quart soufflé dish (see page 54 for instructions on doing this), a Bundt pan, or some other decorative mold or container. Refrigerate for at least 4 hours before serving. See the instructions on page 55 for uncollaring and unmolding.

MAKES TWELVE ¾-CUP SERVINGS

Lime Mousse:

Substitute one 12-ounce can of frozen limeade concentrate for the lemonade concentrate and grated lime rind for the lemon rind.

Each serving contains approximately: Calories: 80;
Grams of fat: negligible; Cholesterol: 1 mg; Sodium: 35 mg

Piña Colada Mousse

This tropical-tasting "lighter than air" dessert is fabulous following an Asian meal of any type. I also like to serve it as an appetizer for brunch in place of a more traditional cold fruit soup.

One 12-ounce can evaporated skim milk, very cold
One 12-ounce can frozen unsweetened pineapple juice concentrate
2 envelopes unflavored gelatin
¼ cup cool water
¼ cup boiling water

3 tablespoons sugar
2 teaspoons pure vanilla extract
2 teaspoons pure coconut extract

1. Several hours before you plan to make the mousse, place the can of milk in the refrigerator. Place a large stainless-steel, glass, or ceramic bowl and the beaters to an electric mixer in the freezer. Place the can of frozen pineapple juice in the refrigerator to thaw, but remain cold.

2. Soften the gelatin in the cool water for 5 minutes. Add the boiling water and stir until the gelatin is completely dissolved. Combine the cold thawed pineapple juice, sugar, extracts, and dissolved gelatin mixture in a small bowl and mix well. Place the bowl in the refrigerator while you whip the milk.

3. Remove the bowl and beaters from the freezer. Pour the cold milk in the bowl and beat until soft peaks form. Remove the pineapple juice mixture from the refrigerator (it should have a syrupy consistency) and, using a rubber spatula, carefully fold it into the whipped milk until no streaks of white show. Pour the mixture into either a collared 1-quart soufflé dish (see page 54 for instructions on doing this), a Bundt pan, or some other decorative mold or container. Refrigerate for at least 4 hours before serving. See page 55 for instructions on uncollaring and unmolding.

MAKES TWELVE ¾-CUP SERVINGS

Each serving contains approximately: Calories: 54;
Grams of fat: negligible; Cholesterol: 1 mg; Sodium: 34 mg

Margarita Mousse

This is another mousse that makes an unusual appetizer for lunch or brunch as well as a delightfully different dessert. It is particularly good served with a Southwestern menu.

One 12-ounce can evaporated skim milk, very cold
One 10-ounce can frozen margarita mix
2 envelopes unflavored gelatin
¼ cup cool water
¼ cup boiling water

1. Several hours before you plan to make the mousse, place the can of milk in the refrigerator. Place a large stainless-steel, glass, or ceramic bowl and the beaters to an electric mixer in the freezer. Place the can of frozen margarita mix in the refrigerator to thaw, but remain cold.

2. Soften the gelatin in the cool water for 5 minutes. Add the boiling water and stir until the gelatin is completely dissolved. Combine the cold thawed margarita mix and dissolved gelatin mixture in a bowl and mix well. Place the bowl in the refrigerator while you whip the milk.

3. Remove the bowl and beaters from the freezer. Pour the cold milk in the bowl and beat until soft peaks form. Remove the margarita mix mixture from the refrigerator (it should have a syrupy consistency) and, using a rubber spatula, carefully fold it thoroughly into the whipped milk, until there are no white streaks. Pour the mixture into either a collared 1-quart soufflé dish (see page 54 for instructions on doing this), a Bundt pan, or some other decorative mold or container. Refrigerate for at least 4 hours before serving. See page 55 for instructions on uncollaring and unmolding.

MAKES TWELVE ⅔-CUP SERVINGS

Each serving contains approximately: Calories: 72;
Grams of fat: negligible; Cholesterol: 1 mg; Sodium: 38 mg

Peanut Butter Mousse

I created this dessert a couple of years ago as a special Valentine's Day column saluting the Peanut Butter Lover's Club of America. It was designed to take us all on a nostalgic trip back to those happy days of childhood when nothing compared with a good peanut butter and jelly sandwich and a glass of cold milk. This mousse, accompanied by jelly-frosted hearts of banana bread, or whole-grain bread, is a more sophisticated version of this tasty and satisfying trio.

One 12-ounce can evaporated skim milk, very cold
2 envelopes unflavored gelatin
¼ cup cool water
¼ cup boiling water
1 cup low-fat ricotta cheese
½ cup unhomogenized (old-fashioned) peanut butter
¼ cup plus 2 tablespoons sugar
1 teaspoon pure vanilla extract
1 tablespoon finely chopped peanuts

1. Several hours before you plan to make the mousse, put the can of milk in the refrigerator. Place a glass, ceramic, or stainless-steel mixing bowl and the beaters to an electric mixer in the freezer so they will be very cold for beating the cold canned milk.

2. Soften the gelatin in the cool water. Add the boiling water, stir until the gelatin is completely dissolved, and set aside.

3. In a food processor combine the cheese, peanut butter, and ¼ cup of the sugar. Blend until smooth. Add the vanilla and dissolved gelatin and blend again until thoroughly mixed. Pour into a glass, enamel, or stainless-steel mixing bowl and refrigerate until it reaches a syrupy consistency.

4. Remove the bowl and beaters from the freezer and beat the evaporated milk until it starts to thicken. Add the remaining 2 tablespoons sugar and continue beating until soft peaks form and

the milk has increased at least four times in volume. Carefully fold the whipped milk into the peanut butter mixture until no streaks of white show. Pour the mousse into a 1-quart collared soufflé dish (see page 54 for instructions on how to do this) and refrigerate for several hours or overnight before serving.

5. To serve, sprinkle the top with the chopped peanuts and carefully remove the waxed-paper collar, following the instructions on page 55.

MAKES TWELVE ⅔-CUP SERVINGS

Each serving contains approximately: Calories: 142;
Grams of fat: 7; Cholesterol: 7 mg; Sodium: 59 mg

Grand Marnier Soufflé

In my opinion this is the queen of soufflés, and the incredibly easy and truly sensational sauce makes it even more regal!

FOR THE SAUCE

1 cup vanilla ice milk, melted
1½ teaspoons Grand Marnier or other orange-flavored liqueur

FOR THE SOUFFLÉ

2 tablespoons corn oil margarine
2½ tablespoons all-purpose unbleached flour
One 12-ounce can evaporated skim milk, heated to the boiling point
2 large egg yolks
⅓ cup sugar
3 tablespoons Grand Marnier or other orange-flavored liqueur
2 teaspoons pure vanilla extract
6 large egg whites
⅛ teaspoon salt
⅛ teaspoon cream of tartar

1. To make the sauce, combine the melted ice milk and Grand Marnier and mix well. Cover and set aside.

2. Melt the margarine in a large saucepan over medium heat. Add the flour and stir constantly for 2 minutes, being careful not to brown. Remove from the heat and add the scalded milk all at once, stirring with a wire whisk. Reduce the heat to low and return the pan to the stove. Bring to a boil and simmer over medium heat until thickened. Remove from the heat and add the egg yolks, one at a time, stirring each one in thoroughly. Add the sugar, Grand Marnier, and vanilla, mix well, and set aside.

3. Preheat the oven to 400°F. In a large bowl, beat the egg whites until frothy. Add the salt and cream of tartar and continue beating until stiff but not dry peaks form. Mix one third of the egg whites into the mixture to lighten it. Gently fold the remaining egg whites into the mixture, being careful not to overmix.

4. Pour the mixture into an 8-inch (6-cup) soufflé dish and place it in the center of the oven. Immediately reduce the oven temperature to 375°F. Cook until the souffé billows and is lightly browned, about 20 minutes. Serve immediately, spooning it onto plates or into small bowls. Spoon 2 tablespoons of the sauce over each serving.

MAKES EIGHT ¾-CUP SERVINGS

Each serving contains approximately: Calories: 163; Grams of fat: 4.8; Cholesterol: 54 mg; Sodium: 149 mg

Chocolate Soufflé

For many people there is no dessert more opulent than a billowing chocolate soufflé, and this one is quite easy to make. I like to undercook a soufflé just slightly so that the center is still a bit runny and almost like a sauce.

One 12-ounce can evaporated skim milk
2 tablespoons cornstarch
⅓ cup unsweetened cocoa powder
¾ cup sugar
½ teaspoon ground cinnamon
1 teaspoon pure vanilla extract
Corn oil margarine
Confectioners' sugar
4 large egg whites
½ teaspoon cream of tartar

1. Combine the evaporated milk and cornstarch in a heavy saucepan or in the top of a double boiler and stir until the cornstarch is completely dissolved. Add the cocoa, ½ cup of the sugar, and the cinnamon and mix well. Cook over medium–low heat (or simmering water), stirring frequently, until the mixture comes to a boil. Continue to cook, stirring constantly, until thickened, about 5 minutes.

2. Remove from the heat and stir in the vanilla. Place plastic wrap over the top of the pan to keep a film from forming. Set aside.

3. Lightly grease the inside of an 8-inch (6–cup) soufflé dish with corn oil margarine. Dust the inside of the greased dish lightly with confectioners' sugar. Preheat the oven to 400°F.

4. Beat the egg whites in a large bowl with an electric mixer on low speed until frothy. Add the cream of tartar and gradually increase the mixer speed to high. Continue beating until soft peaks form. Slowly add the remaining ¼ cup sugar and beat until stiff but not dry peaks form.

5. Stir one quarter of the beaten egg whites into the warm chocolate mixture to lighten it. Add the remaining egg whites to the chocolate and gently fold them in, being careful not to overmix. Spoon the mixture into the soufflé dish.

6. Bake for 15 minutes. It should be puffed up but the center should be a bit runny. Dust the top with confectioners' sugar and serve immediately, spooning it out onto plates or into small bowls.

MAKES SIX ¾-CUP SERVINGS

Each serving contains approximately: Calories: 183; Grams of fat: 1.3; Cholesterol: 2 mg; Sodium: 126 mg

Southern Sweet Potato Soufflé

This is a wonderful winter dessert. It is also a good side dish with holiday-type meals.

4 pounds sweet potatoes, boiled in water to cover until tender, drained, and peeled
¼ cup (½ stick) corn oil margarine, melted
¾ cup nonfat liquid egg substitute
½ cup sugar or honey
¼ cup frozen unsweetened orange juice concentrate, thawed
½ cup nonfat milk
1 tablespoon peeled and grated fresh ginger
1 cup pecans, chopped
1½ tablespoons grated lemon rind
1½ tablespoons grated orange rind
Pinch salt
6 large egg whites

1. Preheat the oven to 400°F. In a large bowl, mash the potatoes. Beat with an electric mixer to remove all the lumps. Beat in the margarine. Beat in the egg substitute until the consistency is

smoother, about 5 minutes. Stir in the sugar, concentrate, milk, ginger, pecans, citrus rinds, and salt.

2. In another large bowl, beat the egg whites with an electric mixer until stiff but not dry peaks form, then fold them into the potato mixture until no streaks of white show. Pour the batter into a 2-quart soufflé dish or a casserole sprayed with nonstick vegetable spray.

3. Bake until a knife inserted in the center of the soufflé comes out clean, 40 to 45 minutes. It will not puff up like a dessert soufflé. Serve immediately, spooning it onto plates or into small bowls.

MAKES EIGHT 1-CUP SERVINGS

Each serving contains approximately: Calories: 360; Grams of fat: 9; Cholesterol: 1 mg; Sodium: 126 mg

Pumpkin Soufflé

If you have been trying to find a recipe for a killer holiday dessert to impress your family and friends, this luscious, light, and cholesterol-free soufflé is just what you're looking for. I suggest making it in a casserole rather than a soufflé dish because the pumpkin texture is heavy enough to fall over the edges of a straight-sided dish as it rises. In fact, it happened to me the first time I made this soufflé and I had a terrible mess in the bottom of my oven. If you have any soufflé left over, cover and refrigerate it to serve the next day as pumpkin pudding.

3 tablespoons corn oil margarine
3 tablespoons all-purpose unbleached flour
One 12-ounce can evaporated skim milk, heated to the boiling point
½ cup sugar
¼ teaspoon salt
2 teaspoons ground cinnamon

½ teaspoon freshly grated nutmeg
¼ teaspoon ground ginger
⅛ teaspoon ground cloves
2 teaspoons pure vanilla extract
One 16-ounce can solid pack pumpkin
6 large egg whites
¼ teaspoon cream of tartar

1. Preheat the oven to 400°F. Melt the margarine in a large saucepan over medium heat. Add the flour and stir constantly for 2 minutes, being careful not to brown. Remove from the heat and add the scalded milk all at once, stirring with a wire whisk. Return the pan to the stove and reduce the heat to low. Bring to a boil and simmer until thickened, 2 to 3 minutes. Remove from the heat, add the remaining ingredients except the egg whites and cream of tartar, and mix well. Set aside.

2. In a large bowl, beat the egg whites with an electric mixer until frothy. Add the cream of tartar and continue beating until stiff but not dry peaks form. Mix one third of the egg whites into the pumpkin mixture to lighten it. Gently fold the remaining egg whites into the mixture, being careful not to overmix.

3. Pour the mixture into a 3-quart casserole and place it in the center of the oven. Immediately reduce the oven temperature to 375°F. Cook until the soufflé billows and is lightly browned, about 30 minutes. Serve immediately, spooning it out onto plates or into small bowls.

MAKES EIGHT ⅔-CUP SERVINGS

Each serving contains approximately: Calories: 166; Grams of fat: 4.5;
Cholesterol: 2 mg; Sodium: 167 mg

Southern Gentleman's Omelet

Dessert omelets are very popular in many regions of France. However, they are all made with whole eggs and generous amounts of butter. This Southern version of an American dessert omelet is much lower in fat and totally cholesterol-free.

> ¼ cup nonfat liquid egg substitute
> 2 tablespoons firmly packed dark brown sugar
> 3 tablespoons Gentleman Jack Rare Tennessee Sipping Whiskey
> 3 large egg whites
> 1 tablespoon corn oil margarine

1. Combine the egg substitute, sugar, and whiskey in a large bowl and whisk until well blended.

2. In another large bowl, beat the egg whites with an electric mixer until stiff but not dry peaks form. Fold the beaten egg whites into the egg substitute mixture until no streaks of white show.

3. In a large omelet pan or nonstick skillet with gently sloping sides, melt the margarine over medium-high heat. Pour the omelet mixture into the pan, rolling the pan so that the mixture is evenly spread over the entire inner surface. Cook until golden brown on the bottom, about 1 minute. Carefully slide the omelet halfway out of the pan onto a large serving dish and, using the lip of the pan, gently fold the remaining half over the top into a classic omelet fold.

MAKES 2 ENTRÉE SERVINGS OR 4 DESSERT SERVINGS

Each serving contains approximately:

	Entrée	Dessert
Calories:	181	91
Grams of fat:	6.7	4
Cholesterol:	0	0
Sodium:	140 mg	70 mg

Pies, Tarts, Turnovers, and Strudels

When making pies and tarts, most of the fat is usually found in the crust. For that reason, I rarely call for a top crust in any of my pie recipes. In a few of the recipes in this section you will find that a lattice top crust is optional, and you may want to use it on special occasions for a prettier presentation. However, you get basically the same taste, with fewer calories, when eating a piece of pie with only a bottom crust.

Rather than making the rich dough usually called for in turnovers and strudels, I routinely use phyllo pastry. It is much lighter, faster, and easier to use and in truth, I really like it better.

Mom's Apple Pie

This all-American favorite is perfect for potluck parties. It is easy to transport and its popularity with all age groups makes it a sure hit at any gathering.

For the crust

3 cups all-purpose unbleached flour
1 tablespoon sugar
¾ teaspoon salt
⅔ cup canola oil
4 to 6 tablespoons nonfat milk

For the filling

About 2 pounds Granny Smith or other tart green apples (5 or 6
    medium-size), peeled, cored, and thinly sliced (6 cups)
⅔ cup sugar
2 tablespoons all-purpose unbleached flour
1 teaspoon ground cinnamon
⅛ teaspoon freshly grated nutmeg
1 tablespoon fresh lemon juice
1 teaspoon grated lemon rind
1 tablespoon corn oil margarine, cut into bits

1. Preheat the oven to 400°F. For the crust, combine the flour, sugar, and salt in a large bowl. Add the oil and mix with a pastry blender or a fork until crumbly. Sprinkle ¼ cup of the milk over the crumbs and stir until the mixture begins to hold together, adding more milk if necessary. Divide the dough in half and form into two balls.

2. Place one ball on a lightly floured surface and roll out to ⅛ inch thick. Place the crust in a 9-inch pie plate and trim ½ inch beyond the edge of the plate. Roll the second ball out to ⅛ inch thick. Using a sharp knife, cut it into ½-inch strips and set aside while making the filling.

3. Combine all the filling ingredients except the margarine in a large bowl. Pour into the crust and dot with the margarine.

4. Lay the pastry strips over the filled pie at ½-inch intervals. Weave through cross strips at a 90-degree angle, folding back alternate strips when weaving. Trim the strips even with the outer rim of the pie plate. Fold the lower crust over the strips, seal, and flute the edge.

5. Bake until the crust is golden brown and the filling bubbly, about 50 minutes. Serve warm with fat-reduced sharp cheddar cheese or vanilla ice milk or frozen yogurt, if desired.

MAKES ONE 9-INCH PIE; 8 SERVINGS

Apple and Cheddar Cheese Pie:

Add 1 cup grated fat-reduced cheddar cheese to the filling mixture in step 3.

Each serving contains approximately: Calories: 340; Grams of fat: 18.7; Cholesterol: 0; Sodium: 228 mg

Dutch Apple Pie

4 medium-size Golden Delicious apples, peeled, cored, and sliced
1 tablespoon fresh lemon juice
¼ cup firmly packed light brown sugar
3 tablespoons all-purpose unbleached flour
1 teaspoon ground cinnamon
¼ teaspoon freshly grated nutmeg
One 9-inch graham cracker crust, unbaked (page 88)

FOR THE TOPPING

¾ cup all-purpose unbleached flour
¼ cup firmly packed light brown sugar
¼ cup (½ stick) corn oil margarine

1. Preheat the oven to 375°F. Combine the apples, lemon juice, brown sugar, flour, cinnamon, and nutmeg. Mix well and turn into the pie shell.

2. Combine the flour and brown sugar for the topping. Cut in the margarine with a fork until pea-sized crumbs form. Sprinkle evenly over the apple mixture.

3. Place the pie on a baking sheet (it can boil over) in the center of the oven and bake until the top is golden and the filling bubbling, about 50 minutes. Cool on a wire rack. Serve at room temperature.

MAKES ONE 9-INCH PIE; 8 SERVINGS

Each serving contains approximately: Calories: 219; Grams of fat: 7.6; Cholesterol: 0; Sodium: 77 mg

Cherry Pie

One 16-ounce package frozen unsweetened pitted dark cherries, thawed
¼ cup all-purpose unbleached flour
2 tablespoons fresh lemon juice
½ teaspoon pure almond extract
½ cup sugar
1 Perfect Pie Crust (recipe follows), unbaked
1 teaspoon cold corn oil margarine, cut into small pieces

Preheat the oven to 350°F. Combine all the filling ingredients in a large bowl and mix well. Spoon the mixture into the unbaked pie crust and dot the top with the margarine. Bake until the crust is nicely browned, about 1 hour.

MAKES ONE 9-INCH PIE; 8 SERVINGS

Each serving contains approximately: Calories: 219; Grams of fat: 7.6; Cholesterol: 0; Sodium: 77 mg

Perfect Pie Crust

I call this pie crust perfect because it is the easiest, fastest pie crust I know—you don't even have to roll it out, you just press it into the pie pan. I feel sure you'll agree with me that this is the simplest way to make pie crust!

1 cup whole-wheat pastry flour
¼ teaspoon salt
¼ cup corn oil
3 tablespoons ice water

1. Preheat the oven to 375°F.

2. Combine the flour and salt in a 9-inch pie pan and mix well.

3. Measure the oil in a large measuring cup. Add the water to the oil and mix well, using a fork.

4. Slowly add the liquid to the flour mixture in the pie pan, mixing it with the same fork. Continue mixing until all the ingredients are well blended. Press onto the bottom and sides of the pan with your fingertips. Make sure that the crust covers the entire inner surface of the pie pan evenly.

5. Prick the bottom of the crust in several places with a fork and bake until golden brown, 20 to 25 minutes. (If the recipe doesn't call for a prebaked crust, omit this step.)

MAKES ONE 9-INCH PIE CRUST; 8 SERVINGS

Perfect Bran Pie Crust:

Replace ¼ cup of the whole-wheat pastry flour with ¼ cup unprocessed wheat bran. Subtract 23 calories per serving.

Each serving contains approximately: Calories: 116; Grams of fat: 7.1; Cholesterol: 0; Sodium: 75 mg

Light and Fresh Cranberry Pecan Pie

This recipe is a revision of an even richer pie. I was able to significantly reduce the calories, cut the fat in half, and eliminate the cholesterol completely from the original recipe and still have a truly delicious and unusual dessert. However, it is still a relatively high-calorie pie. To further cut the number of calories per serving, you may want to make it in a 9-inch-square pan and cut it into 16 square servings instead of 12 pie-shaped wedges.

FOR THE GRAHAM-CRACKER CRUST
2 tablespoons corn oil margarine, melted
1 cup graham cracker crumbs (14 squares, crushed)
2 tablespoons sugar
1 tablespoon nonfat milk

FOR THE FILLING
Two 1-ounce squares semisweet chocolate
½ cup (1 stick) corn oil margarine
2 cups fresh cranberries or unsweetened frozen cranberries, thawed
2 tablespoons firmly packed light brown sugar
⅓ cup chopped pecans
1 tablespoon dry sherry or brandy
2 large egg whites
Pinch salt
⅔ cup granulated sugar
1 cup all-purpose unbleached flour

FOR THE GARNISH
¼ cup unsweetened shredded coconut
¼ cup pecan halves

1. Preheat the oven to 325°F. To make the crust, combine the melted margarine, crumbs, and sugar in a small bowl. Stir in the milk to moisten. Press the mixture firmly in the bottom of a 9- or 10-inch pie pan sprayed with nonstick vegetable spray.

2. To make the filling, melt the chocolate and margarine together in a saucepan over very low heat. Spread the cranberries

evenly over the crust and sprinkle with the brown sugar, chopped nuts, and sherry. Beat the egg whites and salt together with an electric mixer until frothy. Gradually add the white sugar and continue beating until stiff peaks form. Gently stir the melted chocolate mixture and flour into the egg whites and pour over the cranberries.

3. Sprinkle the top with the coconut and decorate with the pecans. Bake just until the center does not wiggle, 40 to 50 minutes. Serve warm.

MAKES ONE 10-INCH PIE; 12 SERVINGS

Each serving contains approximately: Calories: 337; Grams of fat: 17; Cholesterol: 0; Sodium: 250 mg

Blueberry Pie

The grated fresh lemon rind and the touch of nutmeg in the crust of this pie give it a delightfully different flavor which I like very much.

FOR THE CRUST
2 cups all-purpose unbleached flour
1 tablespoon sugar
½ teaspoon salt
1 teaspoon grated lemon rind
½ teaspoon freshly grated nutmeg
½ cup (1 stick) corn oil margarine
4 to 6 tablespoons water
1 tablespoon fresh lemon juice

FOR THE FILLING
4 cups fresh blueberries, picked over and rinsed, or frozen unsweetened
  blueberries, thawed
⅔ cup sugar
3 tablespoons all-purpose unbleached flour
Dash salt
1 teaspoon fresh lemon juice

1. To make the crust, combine the flour, sugar, salt, lemon rind, nutmeg, and margarine in a medium-size bowl and mix with a pastry blender or a fork until crumbly. Add 4 tablespoons of the water and the lemon juice and stir until moist clumps form. If necessary, add another 1 or 2 tablespoons of water to make it hold together. Divide the dough in half and form each half into a ball. Roll one of the balls out on a floured surface into a 12-inch round and place it on a 9-inch glass pie plate. Roll out the second ball to another 12-inch round, then gently roll it up and set it aside. Preheat the oven to 400°F.

2. To make the filling, combine the blueberries, sugar, flour, and salt in a medium-size bowl and mix thoroughly. Spoon the filling into the pie plate and sprinkle with the lemon juice. Cover the top with the other pie crust and make slits in the top for the steam to escape. Bake until the crust is golden brown, 35 to 40 minutes.

MAKES ONE 9-INCH PIE; 8 SERVINGS

Strawberry Pie:

Substitute strawberries for the blueberries and omit the nutmeg in the crust.

Each serving contains approximately: Calories: 343; Grams of fat: 12; Cholesterol: 0; Sodium: 154 mg

Pear Tarte Tatin

Tarte Tatin is usually made with apples, but pears make an even moister version of this famous upside-down pie. The original recipe for Tarte Tatin was created by two French sisters who were forced to earn their living by baking and selling their father's favorite dessert. Their secret was cooking the fruit in the sugar until it caramelized. I am certain that my recipe is much lower in fat than theirs was and it is still absolutely delicious. It is also cholesterol-free!

FOR THE CRUST

½ cup whole-wheat flour
½ cup all-purpose unbleached flour
1 tablespoon confectioners' sugar
¼ teaspoon salt
2½ tablespoons ice water
6 tablespoons (¾ stick) corn oil margarine

FOR THE FILLING

2 pounds ripe pears, preferably Bartlett (about 4 or 5 pears)
¼ cup (½ stick) corn oil margarine
½ cup firmly packed dark brown sugar

1. To make the crust, combine all the crust ingredients in a food processor and mix, using a dough blade, until a ball is formed. Place the dough ball, covered, in the refrigerator to chill about 1 hour.

2. To make the filling, peel the pears, then cut them into halves lengthwise. Carefully remove the center cores. In a heavy ovenproof skillet about 6 inches in diameter and 2½ inches deep, melt the margarine over medium heat. Add the brown sugar and bring to a boil. Reduce the heat to low and simmer for 5 minutes. Remove from the heat and allow to cool until safe to handle.

3. Arrange as many pear halves upright as will fit in a tight circle around the outer edge of the pan as close to each other as possible. Fill in the center with the remaining pear halves. Cook over medium heat until the sugar mixture begins to bubble up between the pears. At this point, reduce the heat to low to prevent the mixture from boiling over. Continue to simmer until the pears can be easily pierced with a fork, about 10 minutes. Do not overcook or the pears will become mushy. Remove from the heat and allow to cool to room temperature, or refrigerate to hasten this step.

4. Preheat the oven to 375°F. Remove the dough from the refrigerator and roll it out into a circle slightly larger in diameter than the skillet. Place the dough over the cooked pears and carefully push it down around the edges between the pears and the side of

the skillet. Trim off any excess dough that sticks above the top of the skillet. Punch holes in the top with the tines of a fork to let steam escape and bake until the crust is golden brown, 25 to 30 minutes. Remove from the oven and allow to cool on a rack for 30 minutes.

5. To serve, turn the pan upside down onto a serving plate. If any of the pears stick to the bottom of the pan, just remove them and place them back in the tarte. Cut the tarte into 6 pie-shaped wedges.

MAKES 6 SERVINGS

Each serving contains approximately: Calories: 398; Grams of fat: 19.8; Cholesterol: 0; Sodium: 105 mg

Banana Cream Pie

This pie is also good in a graham cracker crust. And if you don't want a crust at all, the filling makes a wonderful banana custard.

FOR THE CUSTARD

½ cup sugar
3 tablespoons cornstarch
¼ teaspoon salt
⅓ cup nonfat liquid egg substitute
2 cups nonfat milk
1½ teaspoons pure vanilla extract
1½ cups sliced ripe bananas (¾ pound or 2 small)
One 9-inch pie shell, prebaked

FOR THE MERINGUE

3 large egg whites
½ teaspoon pure vanilla extract
¼ teaspoon cream of tartar
¼ cup sugar

1. To make the custard, mix thoroughly in a saucepan the sugar, cornstarch, salt, and egg substitute. Gradually stir in the milk until smooth. Cook and stir over medium heat until bubbly, then continue cooking until thickened, about 3 more minutes. Remove from the heat and stir in the vanilla.

2. Place the sliced bananas in the bottom of the pie shell and cover the bananas with the hot custard. Set aside.

3. Preheat the oven to 350°F. To make the meringue, beat the egg whites with the vanilla and cream of tartar with an electric mixer until soft peaks form. Gradually add the sugar, beating until stiff, glossy peaks form and all the sugar is dissolved.

4. Spread the meringue over the warm custard, sealing to the edge of the pastry. Bake until the meringue is a golden brown, 12 to 15 minutes. Cool thoroughly, away from a draft, before serving.

MAKES ONE 9-INCH PIE; 8 SERVINGS

Each serving contains approximately: Calories: 254; Grams of fat: 8; Cholesterol: 1 mg; Sodium: 289 mg

Peachy Cream Pie

1 graham cracker pie crust, prebaked (page 88)
1 envelope unflavored gelatin
2 tablespoons cold water
¼ cup boiling water
¾ cup low-fat cottage cheese
¼ cup low-fat milk
1½ teaspoons pure vanilla extract
½ teaspoon pure almond extract
2 tablespoons sugar
2 cups peeled, pitted, and finely chopped peaches (3 large peaches)
Ground cinnamon for garnish

1. Set the baked crust aside to cool to room temperature.

2. Soften the gelatin in the cold water for 5 minutes in a small bowl. Add the boiling water and stir until the gelatin is completely dissolved.

3. Put the gelatin mixture in a blender, add the remaining ingredients, except the peaches and garnish, and blend thoroughly.

4. Add ½ cup of the peaches and blend until smooth. Pour the mixture into a bowl. Add the remaining peaches and mix well. Pour the mixture into the pie crust, sprinkle with cinnamon, and refrigerate until firm, about 3 hours.

MAKES ONE 9-INCH PIE; 8 SERVINGS

Each serving contains approximately: Calories: 220; Grams of fat: 8.8; Cholesterol: 2 mg; Sodium: 282 mg

Rhubarb Meringue Torte

Rhubarb is often called the pie plant and this particular recipe is a real winner in the rhubarb pie category. It is a revision of a recipe that called for four egg yolks, ½ pound butter, and 1 ½ cups sugar. Amazingly enough, this lighter version is even more delicious because you can really taste the subtle flavor of the rhubarb.

FOR THE CRUST
1½ cups all-purpose unbleached flour
½ cup (1 stick) chilled corn oil margarine
1 tablespoon sugar
¼ teaspoon salt

FOR THE FILLING
1 pound fresh rhubarb, washed, leaves removed, and stems finely diced (3½ cups)
¼ cup nonfat liquid egg substitute
½ cup canned evaporated skim milk

½ cup frozen unsweetened apple juice concentrate, thawed
1 teaspoon pure vanilla extract
½ cup sugar
2 tablespoons all-purpose unbleached flour

FOR THE MERINGUE

4 large egg whites
½ cup sugar
1 teaspoon pure vanilla extract

1. Preheat the oven to 350°F. Spray a 9 x 13-inch baking dish with nonstick vegetable spray. Combine the crust ingredients in a medium-size bowl and, using a fork or pastry blender, blend the ingredients until the dough mixture resembles small peas. Press the dough into the prepared pan and bake until a golden brown, about 15 minutes. Remove from the oven and set aside.

2. Spread the diced rhubarb over the baked pie shell. In a saucepan, combine the remaining filling ingredients. Mix well with a wire whisk while bringing the mixture to a boil over medium heat. Stir constantly until thickened. Pour the mixture over the rhubarb and bake until the rhubarb is nearly tender, about 20 minutes.

3. While the rhubarb is baking, make the meringue. In a medium-size bowl, beat the egg whites with an electric mixer until frothy. Add the sugar, 1 tablespoon at a time, beating just until stiff peaks form. Do not allow them to become dry. Beat in the vanilla. Top the rhubarb with the meringue and bake until a golden brown, about 10 minutes more.

MAKES 12 SERVINGS

Each serving contains approximately: Calories: 242; Grams of fat: 8; Cholesterol: negligible; Sodium: 196 mg

Pineapple Pie

FOR THE GRAHAM CRACKER CRUST

FOR THE GRAHAM CRACKER CRUST
2 teaspoons corn oil margarine
2 tablespoons water
1 cup graham cracker crumbs (14 squares)

FOR THE FILLING
1 envelope unflavored gelatin
2 tablespoons cool water
¼ cup boiling water
½ cup low-fat cottage cheese
¼ cup nonfat milk
1 teaspoon pure vanilla extract
1 tablespoon sugar
2 cups crushed pineapple packed in natural juice, well drained
Ground cinnamon for garnish

1. Preheat the oven to 250°F. Combine all the ingredients for the crust in a 9-inch pie pan. Mix well and pat out evenly to form the crust. Bake for 15 minutes. Cool on a rack.

2. Combine the gelatin and cool water in a small bowl and allow to stand for 5 minutes to soften. Add the boiling water and stir until the gelatin is completely dissolved.

3. Combine the remaining filling ingredients in a blender until smooth. Add the dissolved gelatin and blend until smooth. Pour the mixture into the cooled pie crust. Sprinkle the top with cinnamon and refrigerate until firm, about 3 hours.

MAKES ONE 9-INCH PIE; 12 SERVINGS

Piña Colada Pie:

Add 1 teaspoon pure coconut extract to the blender with the other ingredients in step 3.

Each serving contains approximately: Calories: 76; Grams of fat: 1.4; Cholesterol: 1 mg; Sodium: 89 mg

Pineapple Pumpkin Pie

1 Graham Cracker Pie Crust and Topping, prebaked (recipe follows)
2 envelopes unflavored gelatin
3 tablespoons cold water
1/4 cup boiling water
One 16-ounce can solid pack pumpkin
One 8-ounce can crushed pineapple in natural juice, undrained
4 ripe dates, pitted and chopped (1/4 cup)
1 cup nonfat milk
1 1/2 teaspoons ground cinnamon
1/4 teaspoon ground ginger
1/8 teaspoon ground cloves
2 teaspoons pure vanilla extract

1. Set the baked crust aside to cool to room temperature.

2. Soften the gelatin in the cold water for 5 minutes in a small bowl. Add the boiling water and stir until the gelatin is completely dissolved.

3. Put the gelatin mixture and the remaining ingredients in a blender and blend until smooth and frothy. Allow the mixture to stand until slightly thickened before pouring into the baked pie shell.

4. Sprinkle the reserved graham cracker crumbs from the pie crust recipe over the top of the pie and chill for at least 3 hours before serving.

MAKES ONE 9-INCH PIE; 8 SERVINGS

Applesauce Pumpkin Pie:

Substitute 1 cup unsweetened applesauce for the crushed pineapple.

Each serving contains approximately: Calories: 226; Grams of fat: 8.6; Cholesterol: 1 mg; Sodium: 271 mg

Graham Cracker Pie Crust
and Topping

16 graham cracker squares
¼ cup (½ stick) corn oil margarine, at room temperature

1. Preheat the oven to 375°F.

2. Put the graham cracker squares in a large plastic bag and crush with a rolling pin until they are fine crumbs.

3. Put the crumbs in a bowl and add the margarine. Using a pastry blender or a fork, mix the crumbs with the margarine until completely mixed and the consistency of a stiff dough. Reserve 2 tablespoons of this mixture to use later.

4. Place the remaining mixture in a 9- or 10-inch pie plate and, with your fingertips, press out evenly over the entire inner surface of the pie plate.

5. Place the reserved 2 tablespoons of the mixture in another baking dish to be baked at the same time as the crust.

6. Bake both the pie crust and reserved crumbs until lightly browned, about 8 minutes.

7. Cool the pie crust to room temperature before adding a filling. Use the 2 tablespoons of the mixture for sprinkling over the top of the filling.

MAKES 1 PIE CRUST; 8 SERVINGS

Cinnamon Graham Cracker Pie Crust
and Topping:

Add ½ teaspoon ground cinnamon to the crumbs and mix thoroughly before adding the margarine.

Chocolate Graham Cracker Pie Crust and Topping:

Use only 14 graham cracker squares and add 2½ tablespoons unsweetened cocoa powder.

Each serving contains approximately: Calories: 168; Grams of fat: 8.4; Cholesterol: 0; Sodium: 190 mg

Key Lime Pie

You can use either fresh lime juice or the bottled Key lime juice available from Florida to make this pie. I usually use fresh lime juice because I have to buy the limes for the fresh grated rind anyway.

1 cup sugar
3 tablespoons cornstarch
1½ cups cold water
2 large egg yolks, lightly beaten
1 tablespoon corn oil margarine
1 tablespoon grated lime rind
¼ cup fresh lime juice
One 9-inch Perfect Pie Crust, prebaked (page 77)
4 large egg whites

1. Preheat the oven to 350°F. In a heavy, 2-quart saucepan, combine ¾ cup of the sugar, the cornstarch, and water and mix until the cornstarch is completely dissolved. Add the egg yolks and mix thoroughly. Bring to a boil over medium heat and allow to boil for 1 minute. Remove from the heat, add the margarine, and mix well. Add the grated lime rind and juice and again mix well. Allow the custard to cool.

2. Spoon the custard into the baked pie shell.

3. Beat the egg whites until frothy, then begin adding the remaining ¼ cup sugar slowly, beating well after each addition. Continue beating until stiff peaks form.

4. Spread the meringue over the custard, being careful to cover the entire surface of the pie, and bake until golden brown, about 15 minutes.

MAKES ONE 9-INCH PIE; 8 SERVINGS

Each serving contains approximately: Calories: 330; Grams of fat: 8; Cholesterol: 53 mg; Sodium: 173 mg

Mincemeat Pie

This is a lighter version of the ever-popular holiday dessert. You can double this recipe, make it in a 9 x 13-inch baking dish, and cut it into small squares for mincemeat "cookies."

¾ cup dark raisins
¾ cup dried currants
¾ cup chopped mixed dried fruit
1 pound Golden Delicious apples (3 medium-size), peeled, cored, and finely chopped (3 cups)
1 tablespoon grated lemon rind
1 teaspoon ground cinnamon
½ teaspoon freshly grated nutmeg
Pinch ground cloves
½ cup firmly packed dark brown sugar
¾ cup apple cider
½ cup dry white wine
One 9-inch Perfect Pie Crust, unbaked (page 77)

1. Mix all the ingredients together except ¼ cup of the apple cider and the crust in a large saucepan. Cook over very low heat for about 3 hours, stirring occasionally. About halfway through the cooking time, add the remaining apple cider.

2. Preheat the oven to 400°F. Remove the mincemeat from the heat and spoon it into the pie crust. Bake until the crust is golden brown, about 25 minutes.

MAKES 3 ½ CUPS FILLING AND ONE 9-INCH PIE; 8 SERVINGS

Each serving contains approximately: Calories: 319; Grams of fat: 7.9;
Cholesterol: 0; Sodium: 147 mg

Microwave Zucchini "Apple" Pie

This is a wonderful recipe for parties because it is both inexpensive and easy to make. Because most people mistake this squash pie for apple, I call it Zucchini "Apple" Pie.

FOR THE FILLING

1½ pounds medium-size zucchini, peeled, halved lengthwise, and cut
*   crosswise into thin slices (4 cups)*
½ cup granulated sugar
⅓ cup firmly packed light brown sugar
¼ cup all-purpose unbleached flour
¼ cup buttermilk
1 tablespoon cider vinegar
1 tablespoon water
1 teaspoon fresh lemon juice
½ teaspoon ground cinnamon
½ teaspoon freshly grated nutmeg
One 9-inch Perfect Pie Crust, prebaked (page 77)

FOR THE CRUMB TOPPING

¼ cup (½ stick) corn oil margarine
⅓ cup firmly packed light brown sugar
⅔ cup all-purpose unbleached flour

1. Place all the filling ingredients in a 2-quart microwave-safe bowl. Stir to mix. Microwave uncovered on High, stirring 3 times, until thickened, 8 to 11 minutes. Pour into the baked pie shell.

2. To make the topping, melt the margarine in a small microwave-safe bowl. Stir in the remaining topping ingredients until blended. Cover with a lid or vented plastic wrap. Microwave on High, stirring twice, until slightly browned and bubbly, 1½ to 2 minutes.

3. Spread out the topping on a piece of aluminum foil. When cool enough to handle, sprinkle evenly over the filled pie. Chill in the refrigerator for at least 3 hours before cutting.

MAKES ONE 9-INCH PIE; 8 SERVINGS

Each serving contains approximately: Calories: 348; Grams of fat: 14; Cholesterol: negligible; Sodium: 221 mg

Bean Pie

This is a revision I did for a reader about a year ago. I thought it was a rather bizarre recipe, but was pleased to find it very tasty and a real conversation piece!

One 9-inch vegetable shortening deep-dish pie crust
2 tablespoons corn oil margarine
2 tablespoons buttermilk
1 cup sugar
1 tablespoon all-purpose unbleached flour
1 tablespoon ground cinnamon
1 large egg plus 4 additional large egg whites or ½ cup nonfat liquid egg substitute plus 1 large egg white
One 15-ounce can navy or Great Northern beans, rinsed, drained, and mashed
1 cup canned evaporated skim milk
½ teaspoon pure vanilla extract

1. Preheat the oven to 400°F. If the crust is frozen, set it out to thaw while making the filling.

2. In a large bowl, combine the margarine, buttermilk, and sugar and blend until smooth and creamy. Add the flour and cinnamon and blend well. Add the egg and egg whites and beat well. Beat in the beans, then the milk and vanilla. Spoon the filling into the thawed crust.

3. Place the pie on a baking sheet (it has the tendency to bubble over) and bake for 5 minutes. Lower the temperature to 325°F and bake until a knife inserted in the center comes out clean, an additional 45 to 50 minutes.

MAKES ONE 9-INCH PIE; 8 SERVINGS

Each serving contains approximately: Calories: 304; Grams of fat: 9;
Cholesterol: 28 mg; Sodium: 234 mg

Mint Pie

1 Graham Cracker Pie Crust and Topping, prebaked (page 88)
1 envelope unflavored gelatin
2 tablespoons cold water
¼ cup boiling water
2 cups nonfat milk
1½ teaspoons pure vanilla extract
¼ teaspoon pure mint extract
2 tablespoons sugar

1. Allow the crust to cool to room temperature.

2. Soften the gelatin in the cold water in a medium-size bowl. Add the boiling water and stir until the gelatin is completely dissolved.

3. Add the milk to the gelatin mixture and mix thoroughly. Place in the refrigerator until the mixture starts to thicken, about 30 minutes.

4. Remove the gelatin mixture from the refrigerator and pour into a blender. Add the extracts and sugar and blend until foamy. Pour into the cooled pie crust. Sprinkle the reserved crumbs evenly over the top and place the pie in the refrigerator to chill for at least 3 hours before serving. If possible, make a day ahead of time.

MAKES ONE 9-INCH PIE; 8 SERVINGS

Variation:

Substitute Chocolate Graham Cracker Pie Crust and Topping (page 89) for the pie crust.

Each serving contains approximately: Calories: 204; Grams of fat: 8.5; Cholesterol: 1 mg; Sodium: 223 mg

Famous Chocolate Cookie Cream Pie

This low-fat recipe is a revision of a significantly higher calorie pie and it tastes much richer than it actually is.

One 9-ounce box chocolate wafer cookies
¼ cup water
24 large marshmallows
½ cup nonfat milk
3 tablespoons sugar
1 cup nonfat ricotta cheese

1. Set aside 5 wafers for garnish. Coarsely chop 10 wafers and set them aside. Roll the remaining wafers into fine crumbs. Place the crumbs in a medium-size bowl, sprinkle with the water, and mix until the crumbs begin to hold together. Spray a 9-inch pie pan with a nonstick vegetable spray, then press the mixture into the pan and set aside.

2. Melt the marshmallows with the milk and sugar in a 2-quart saucepan over medium-low heat, stirring constantly. Set aside to cool slightly.

3. Blend the ricotta cheese in a blender or a food processor until smooth and creamy and fold it into the marshmallow mixture along with the 10 chopped wafers. Pour the mixture into the crust and chill until firm before cutting, about 4 hours. Garnish each serving with half a wafer.

MAKES ONE 9-INCH PIE; 10 SERVINGS

Each serving contains approximately: Calories: 213; Grams of fat: 4; Cholesterol: 13 mg; Sodium: 61 mg

Brownie Pie

....

¼ cup (½ stick) corn oil margarine
⅔ cup firmly packed dark brown sugar
½ cup nonfat liquid egg substitute
¼ cup buttermilk
¼ cup all-purpose unbleached flour
⅓ cup unsweetened cocoa powder
1 teaspoon pure vanilla extract
¼ teaspoon salt

1. Preheat the oven to 400°F. Spray a 9-inch pie plate with a nonstick vegetable spray. Melt the margarine in a saucepan over very low heat. Remove from the heat and stir in the sugar. Cool slightly, then whisk in the remaining ingredients.

2. Pour the batter into the prepared pan and bake for 15 minutes. Decrease the oven temperature to 350°F and bake until set, 5 minutes more. Cool slightly before serving.

MAKES ONE 9-INCH PIE; 8 SERVINGS

Each serving contains approximately: Calories: 163; Grams of fat: 7; Cholesterol: negligible; Sodium: 184 mg

Peanut Butter Pie

This easy to make pie is one of my own favorite desserts. Of course, I have yet to find anything with peanut butter in it that I don't like!

1 envelope unflavored gelatin
2 tablespoons cool water
¼ cup boiling water
1½ cups nonfat milk
½ cup unhomogenized (old-fashioned) creamy peanut butter
3 tablespoons honey
1½ teaspoons pure vanilla extract
One 9-inch graham cracker crust, prebaked (page 88)
Ground cinnamon for garnish

1. In a small bowl, soften the gelatin in the cool water and allow to stand for 5 minutes. Add the boiling water and stir until the gelatin is completely dissolved.

2. Combine the milk, peanut butter, honey, vanilla, and dissolved gelatin in a blender and blend until smooth and frothy. Pour the mixture into the pie shell and sprinkle lightly with cinnamon. Refrigerate until the filling is firm, at least 2 hours.

MAKES ONE 9-INCH PIE; 8 SERVINGS

Each serving contains approximately: Calories: 253; Grams of fat: 15; Cholesterol: 1 mg; Sodium: 28 mg

Nonfat Sour Cream Pie

1 cup dark raisins
1 cup boiling water
¾ cup sugar
6 tablespoons all-purpose unbleached flour
Dash salt

2 cups nonfat milk
⅓ cup nonfat liquid egg substitute
1 cup nonfat sour cream
½ teaspoon pure vanilla extract
One 9-inch pie crust, prebaked (page 77)

3 large egg whites
¼ teaspoon cream of tartar
¼ cup sugar

1. Preheat the oven to 350°F. Place the raisins in a small bowl and cover with the water. Allow to stand for 5 minutes. Drain well and set aside.

2. In a medium-size heavy saucepan, combine the sugar, flour, and salt. Gradually stir in the milk. Bring to a boil over medium heat, stirring constantly. Boil and stir 1 minute. Remove from the heat and stir ½ cup of the hot milk mixture into the egg substitute. Return to the saucepan and cook over low heat 3 minutes, stirring constantly.

3. Remove from the heat and cool slightly. Stir in the sour cream, vanilla, and raisins just until blended. Pour into the baked pie shell and set aside while making the meringue.

4. To make meringue, beat the egg whites with an electric mixer until frothy. Add the cream of tartar, then gradually beat in the sugar until the whites form stiff peaks and are glossy. Spread the meringue over the filling, sealing to the edges. Bake until golden brown, 12 to 15 minutes. Cool on a wire rack and then refrigerate, covered, for 2 to 3 hours before serving.

MAKES ONE 9-INCH PIE; 8 SERVINGS

Each serving contains approximately: Calories: 316; Grams of fat: 6; Cholesterol: 1 mg; Sodium: 246 mg

Buttermilk Pie

This quick and easy one-bowl pie is a fabulous base for fresh fruit desserts. It is delicious served warm with sliced peaches sprinkled with a bit of cinnamon. It also makes a marvelous, if nontraditional, strawberry shortcake.

Instead of making one pie, you can also use this recipe to make eight small tarts. The only change in method is the cooking time, which is slightly shorter for tarts.

½ cup reduced-fat Bisquick
2 tablespoons all-purpose unbleached flour
1¼ cups sugar
1 cup buttermilk
2 tablespoons corn oil margarine, melted
1 large egg
3 large egg whites
1½ teaspoons pure vanilla extract

1. Preheat the oven to 350°F. Spray a 9-inch pie pan with nonstick vegetable spray.

2. Combine the Bisquick, flour, and sugar in a large bowl and mix well. Add the remaining ingredients and mix until smooth. Pour the mixture into the pie pan and bake until a knife inserted in the center comes out clean, about 30 minutes.

MAKES ONE 9-INCH PIE; 8 SERVINGS

Each serving contains approximately: Calories: 221; Grams of fat: 4; Cholesterol: 28 mg; Sodium: 176 mg

NOTE: ½ cup of reduced-fat Bisquick contains: 210 calories, 4 grams of fat, 0 cholesterol, and 660 mg sodium.

Magic Meringue Pie

This is a recipe that I revised for a reader in Akron, Ohio. Even though it is much lighter than the original version, it is still a very creamy-textured and rich-tasting pie.

FOR THE FILLING

¾ *cup sugar*

2 *tablespoons all-purpose unbleached flour*

⅛ *teaspoon salt*

1 *cup light sour cream*

1 *tablespoon fresh lemon juice*

⅓ *cup nonfat liquid egg substitute*

One 20-ounce can crushed pineapple packed in natural juice, drained, reserving ½ cup of the juice

FOR THE MERINGUE

6 *tablespoons sugar*

1 *tablespoon cornstarch*

½ *cup water*

3 *large egg whites*

⅛ *teaspoon salt*

½ *teaspoon pure vanilla extract*

One 9-inch deep dish pie crust, prebaked

1. For the filling, combine the sugar, flour, and salt in a medium-size saucepan and mix well. Stir in the remaining filling ingredients. Cook over medium heat, stirring constantly, until the mixture comes to a boil and thickens, about 4 minutes. Remove from the heat and cover the surface with plastic wrap. Refrigerate until cool, about 1 hour.

2. While the filling is cooling, make the meringue. Combine 2 tablespoons of the sugar and the cornstarch in a small saucepan. Gradually whisk in the water. Cook over medium heat, stirring constantly, until the mixture comes to a boil. Boil for 1 minute. Remove from the heat and allow to come to room temperature.

3. Preheat the oven to 350°F. In a medium-size bowl, beat the egg whites, salt, and vanilla together with an electric mixer until soft peaks form. Gradually beat in the remaining ¼ cup of sugar, 1 tablespoon at a time. Slowly add the cornstarch and water mixture and continue beating until firm peaks form.

4. Pour the cooled filling into the pie crust. Spoon the meringue over the filling, being careful to seal the edges. Bake until the meringue begins to turn golden brown, about 15 minutes. Chill before serving.

MAKES ONE 9-INCH PIE; 8 SERVINGS

Each serving contains approximately: Calories: 345; Grams of fat: 10.7; Cholesterol: 5 mg; Sodium: 288 mg

Fresh Apricot Cobbler

This is a yummy, old-fashioned dessert that I developed for *Cooking Healthy* magazine as a part of a Fresh From the Garden Menu. It is best made in the summertime when fresh apricots are at their peak.

FOR THE DOUGH
1 cup whole-wheat flour
1 cup all-purpose unbleached flour
1½ teaspoons baking powder
¼ teaspoon baking soda
½ teaspoon salt
3 tablespoons cold corn oil margarine
⅔ cup buttermilk

FOR THE FILLING
2 pounds ripe apricots, pitted and quartered (4 cups)
¼ cup firmly packed light brown sugar
1 tablespoon fresh lemon juice

1. To make the dough, combine the flours, baking powder, baking soda, and salt in a large bowl. Add the cold margarine and

cut it into the dry ingredients using a pastry blender or fork. When the dough is crumbly, stir in the buttermilk and mix well.

2. Turn the dough out onto a floured surface and knead for 1 minute. Return the dough to the bowl, cover with a towel, and set aside.

3. Preheat the oven to 400°F. Combine all the filling ingredients in a bowl and mix well. Set aside.

4. Roll out the dough ¼ inch thick. Spray a standard-size loaf pan with a nonstick vegetable spray. Lay the dough in the pan, allowing the edges to hang over the sides. Spoon the apricot mixture on top of the dough and fold the dough edges over the top of the apricots and squeeze them together tightly.

5. Place the cobbler in the oven and bake until the top is a golden brown, about 30 minutes.

MAKES 8 SERVINGS

Fresh Peach Cobbler:

Substitute peeled and pitted peaches for the apricots and add 1 tablespoon ground cinnamon and 2 teaspoons pure vanilla extract in step 3.

Boysenberry Cobbler:

Use 4 cups boysenberries in place of the apricots and substitute ⅓ cup granulated sugar for the brown sugar.

Each serving contains approximately: Calories: 233; Grams of fat: 5.3;
Cholesterol: 1 mg; Sodium: 173 mg

Cinnamon Apple Tarts

These tasty tarts are quick and easy to make and perfect for children to learn how to make themselves. The secret to success when you're using phyllo dough is to follow the package directions when thawing it. Always remove the package from the freezer and put it in the refrigerator to thaw overnight, then remove it from the refrigerator and bring it to room temperature before using it.

2 pounds Golden Delicious apples, peeled, cored, and thinly sliced
2 tablespoons firmly packed brown sugar
3 tablespoons ground cinnamon
2 tablespoons fresh lemon juice
1 tablespoon pure vanilla extract
12 sheets phyllo dough, thawed according to package instructions

1. Preheat the oven to 325°F. Cook the apples, stirring, in a nonstick pan or a pan sprayed with nonstick vegetable spray until the apples are slightly soft. Add the sugar and cinnamon and mix well. Add the lemon juice and vanilla and cook until the apples are soft. Total cooking time should not exceed 10 minutes. Remove from the heat and cool completely.

2. Spray each of the phyllo sheets with nonstick spray and fold in half. Spray again, then fold in half again, then spray again. Each phyllo dough sheet will be one quarter its original size.

3. Place ¼ cup of the apple mixture in the center of each folded sheet and fold all four corners into the center, overlapping them slightly. Turn seam side down and place on a baking sheet sprayed with nonstick spray. Make 3 slits in each tart to allow steam to escape during cooking. Bake until they turn a golden brown, about 15 minutes.

MAKES 12 TARTS

Each tart contains approximately: Calories: 102;
Grams of fat: negligible; Cholesterol: 0; Sodium: 79 mg

Pumpkin Tarts

Phyllo tart shells win in all categories over regular pie crust. They are prettier, lower in fat and calories, and easier to make. The uncooked pumpkin filling in these tarts is also the fastest and easiest I have ever come up with. If you don't want to spend the time making the tarts, just serve the filling in sherbet glasses and call it pumpkin pudding!

FOR THE FILLING

One 16-ounce can solid pack pumpkin
2 cups low-fat ricotta cheese
¼ cup sugar
1 tablespoon ground cinnamon
1 teaspoon ground allspice
¼ teaspoon freshly grated nutmeg
4 teaspoons pure vanilla extract

FOR THE SHELLS

8 sheets phyllo dough, thawed according to package instructions
Ground cinnamon to taste

1. Combine the filling ingredients in a food processor fitted with the metal blade and blend until satin smooth. Refrigerate, covered, several hours or overnight.

2. Preheat the oven to 350°F. Trim the edges off the sheets of phyllo dough to form a square, discarding the remnants. Quarter the resulting squares to form 4 piles of 8 sheets each—you now have 32 small squares.

3. Place 1 square of phyllo dough on the counter, coat with nonstick vegetable spray, and dust lightly with cinnamon. Place a second square on top of the first square, fanning the squares so that all corners are separated from those that have come before. Continue in this way until you have built up 4 layers—this is one tart shell. Repeat to create 8 tart shells.

4. Coat two baking sheets with nonstick vegetable spray. Arrange eight ½-cup ramekins or custard cups, inverted, on top of the baking sheets and coat the outside of each ramekin with nonstick vegetable spray. Place one tart shell on top of each inverted ramekin. Press down onto the sides of the cup. Note: Be sure the tart shells do not overlap or touch, as this will cause them to stick and break when you remove them from the ramekins after baking.

5. Bake until golden brown, about 12 minutes. Remove from the oven, cool slightly, and lift each phyllo shell off its cup, placing it right side up on a serving dish or individual plates. Spoon or pipe ½ cup of the pumpkin filling mixture into each tart shell and serve.

MAKES 8 SERVINGS

Each serving contains approximately: Calories: 197; Grams of fat: 5; Cholesterol: 19 mg; Sodium: 156 mg

Spiced Pear Turnovers

4 large pears, peeled, cored, and sliced (4 cups)
2 tablespoons firmly packed dark brown sugar
2 teaspoons ground cinnamon
¼ teaspoon ground allspice
¼ teaspoon freshly grated nutmeg
2 teaspoons pure vanilla extract
8 sheets phyllo dough, thawed according to package directions

1. Place the pears in a large saucepan. Combine the brown sugar and spices and mix well. Add this mixture to the pears and toss together. Cook over low heat until the sugar has melted and the pears can easily be pierced with the tines of a fork, about 5 minutes. Remove from the heat and stir in the vanilla. Cool to room temperature.

2. Preheat the oven to 375°F. Lay one sheet of the phyllo on a work surface with the narrow end toward you. (Cover the remaining sheets with a damp towel to prevent them from drying out.)

Spray the phyllo with a nonstick vegetable spray. Fold the sheet into thirds lengthwise and spray again. Spoon ¼ cup of the pear mixture about 2 inches from the bottom of the strip. Fold up the 2-inch flap of the phyllo to cover the filling. Fold the lower left hand corner of the phyllo diagonally to the right side, just as if you were starting to fold a flag. Then continue folding diagonally until you reach the end of the sheet. Lift the turnover onto a baking sheet which has either been covered with parchment paper or sprayed with nonstick vegetable spray and spray it again. Repeat the procedure with the remaining sheets of phyllo.

3. Place the turnovers in the center of the oven and bake until golden brown, about 10 minutes.

MAKES 8 TURNOVERS

Apple Turnovers:

Substitute 4 cups sliced Golden Delicious apples for the pears and eliminate the allspice.

Each turnover contains approximately: Calories: 113;
Grams of fat: negligible; Cholesterol: 0; Sodium: 71 mg

Sugar-Free Apple Strudel

2 tablespoons corn oil margarine
4 Golden Delicious apples, peeled, cored, and diced (4 cups)
½ cup dark raisins
4 sheets phyllo dough, thawed according to package instructions
¼ cup almonds, toasted in a 350°F oven until golden brown, 8 to 10
  minutes (optional)

1. Preheat the oven to 375°F. Melt the margarine in a large skillet, add the apples and raisins, and cook over medium heat, stirring frequently, until the apples can easily be pierced with a fork, about 10 minutes. Cool to room temperature.

2. Place one sheet of phyllo, with the wide side toward you, on a piece of parchment paper or a large dry towel and spray with a nonstick vegetable spray. Place a second sheet about 1 inch down from the top of the first sheet and spray again. Continue with the third and fourth sheets, placing each one down about 1 inch from the top of the previous sheet. Spoon the apple mixture about 3 inches up from the bottom, leaving 3 inches of phyllo on all sides. Fold the 3-inch flaps in toward the center and over the apples. Using the parchment paper or towel to help you, roll the strudel evenly in jelly-roll fashion away from you to form the strudel. Again using the parchment or towel to help you, lift the strudel onto a baking sheet which has been covered with parchment paper or sprayed with a nonstick vegetable spray. Spray the rolled strudel and bake until golden brown, 12 to 15 minutes. Remove from the oven and allow to rest for 30 minutes before slicing. To slice, use a very sharp or serrated knife and cut crosswise into 8 equal pieces. Serve warm or cold.

MAKES 8 SERVINGS

Each serving contains approximately: Calories: 120; Grams of fat: 3; Cholesterol: 0; Sodium: 73 mg

Cranberry Strudel

This delicious dessert is perfect for holiday parties and offers a nice change from some of the more usual selections such as mincemeat and pumpkin pies.

¾ cup dried cranberries
¾ cup water
3 large pears, peeled, cored, and diced (3 cups)
½ cup sugar
2 tablespoons cornstarch
1 tablespoon pure vanilla extract
½ teaspoon ground cinnamon
4 graham cracker squares

½ cup pecans halves, toasted in a 350°F oven until golden brown, 8
   to 10 minutes
12 sheets phyllo dough (about ½ package), thawed according to package instructions
Butter-flavored nonstick vegetable spray

1. In a large nonstick skillet, combine the cranberries and water. Simmer over medium heat until the liquid nearly evaporates, 10 to 12 minutes. In a large bowl, combine the pears, sugar, cornstarch, vanilla, and cinnamon. Add to the cranberries and cook over medium-high heat, stirring frequently, for about 10 minutes. The pears should be tender and the mixture very thick. Cool completely.

2. In a food processor, combine the graham crackers and pecans and process to form crumbs. Place a kitchen towel on a work surface. Cover the phyllo dough with a second towel to prevent drying.

3. To assemble the strudel, working with 1 sheet of phyllo dough at a time and keeping the remaining dough covered, place 1 sheet of the phyllo dough on the towel and spray lightly with butter-flavored spray. Top with another sheet of phyllo, lightly spray it, and sprinkle with about 1 tablespoon crumbs. Repeat, using all the remaining phyllo sheets and crumbs.

4. Preheat the oven to 375°F. Spray a large baking sheet with nonstick vegetable spray. Spoon the filling over the dough to within 2 inches of the long edges and 1 inch of the short edges. Using the towel, carefully roll up the strudel from the long side to enclose the filling. Transfer to the prepared baking sheet seam side down.

5. Spray the top of the strudel lightly with the butter-flavored spray. Carefully make 12 shallow equal cuts through the top layers of phyllo but not to the filling. Bake until golden brown, 40 to 45 minutes. Cool 10 minutes before cutting at the scored sections.

MAKES 12 SERVINGS

Each serving contains approximately: Calories: 150; Grams of fat: 3.4;
Cholesterol: 0; Sodium: 71 mg

Fruit Pizza

This is an unusual, tasty, and very pretty dessert. I like to serve it with vanilla ice milk or nonfat frozen yogurt.

½ cup warm water
1 teaspoon active dry yeast (check expiration date on envelope)
3 tablespoons sugar
1½ cups all-purpose unbleached flour
¼ teaspoon salt
1½ teaspoons canola oil
1 teaspoon pure vanilla extract
¼ cup fruit-only strawberry jam
3 ounces part-skim mozzarella cheese, grated (¾ cup)
1½ cups chopped fresh fruit or unsweetened frozen fruit, thawed, such as strawberries, peaches, or blueberries

1. Place the warm water in a small bowl. Sprinkle the yeast and 1 teaspoon of the sugar over the top and stir to combine. Set aside until foamy, about 5 minutes.

2. Combine the remaining sugar, the flour and salt in a medium-size bowl. Stir in the oil, vanilla, and yeast mixture and mix until smooth. Remove the dough to a lightly floured surface and knead until smooth and elastic, about 10 minutes. Place the dough in a bowl sprayed with a nonstick vegetable spray. Turn the dough ball in the bowl so that the top is coated with the spray and cover with a towel. Set aside in a warm place to rise until doubled in bulk, about 45 minutes.

3. Punch the dough down and return it to the floured surface. Knead for 2 minutes and place it back in the sprayed bowl. Allow to rest for 20 minutes. Preheat the oven to 400°F.

4. Roll the dough out into a 12-inch circle and place it either on a nonstick pizza pan or on one sprayed with a nonstick vegetable spray. Top the dough with the strawberry jam, spreading it evenly over the top, but leaving a ½-inch border around the edges. Sprin-

kle the cheese evenly over the jam. Bake for 5 minutes. Remove from the oven and arrange the chopped fruit decoratively over the top. Return to the oven and bake until the crust is golden brown around the edges, an additional 5 minutes. Allow to cool slightly before cutting into 8 pie-shaped wedges.

MAKES 8 SERVINGS

Each serving contains approximately: Calories: 186; Grams of fat: 2.9; Cholesterol: 6 mg; Sodium: 126 mg

Cakes

This is the largest section in the book because it is the category for which I receive the most revision requests. Whether you want to start from scratch or use a mix, you will find lots of wonderful ideas in this chapter.

Pavlova

According to Australian folklore, there was once a time when a young woman was not allowed to be married until she could make a perfect Pavlova—the delicate meringue cake named for the famous ballerina. The trick is to make this meringue firm enough to hold its shape without being so brittle that it shatters and flies off the plate when cut with a fork.

Recently I had the best Pavlova I have ever eaten at a press party for the city of Sydney, Australia, given by Lou Hammond Public Relations in New York. The next day I called Lou and ask her if she could possibly get me the recipe. Much to my surprise she said, "It's my recipe and of course you can have it." So, now we can all make a perfect Pavlova!

In Australia they cover their Pavlovas with whipped cream and fresh fruit. For a lighter dessert I use either nonfat frozen yogurt or vanilla ice milk instead and I like it even better.

5 large egg whites
¼ teaspoon salt
1 cup sugar
4 teaspoons cornstarch
½ teaspoon pure vanilla extract
½ teaspoon white vinegar

1. Position the oven rack in the bottom third of the oven. Preheat the oven to 275°F.

2. Cut a piece of parchment paper to fit the bottom of a baking sheet. Draw a 10-inch circle on the paper by tracing around the bottom of a 10-inch cake pan with a pen. Put the paper on the baking sheet marked side down. You will be able to see the circle through the clean side of the paper. Set aside. (If you don't have parchment paper, you can use a 10-inch pie plate.)

3. In a large, clean bowl beat the egg whites with an electric mixer until they are foamy. Add the salt and continue to beat until stiff peaks form. Continue beating while adding the sugar 1 tablespoon at a time. When all of the sugar has been beaten in, beat in the cornstarch, then the vanilla and vinegar.

4. Place a dab of the meringue mixture under each corner of the paper on the baking sheet to hold it down. Spoon the remaining meringue in the center of the circle drawn on the paper. Using a rubber spatula, carefully spread the meringue to the edge of the circle, leaving a layer of about 1 inch in the center and pushing the excess up at the edges to form a nest. Bake the meringue until the outside is firm, about 1 hour and 15 minutes. The meringue will have little or no color. Remove from the oven and cool on a rack. When cooled, use a large spatula to lift the Pavlova from the paper.

MAKES 10 SERVINGS

Each serving contains approximately: Calories: 91;
Grams of fat: negligible; Cholesterol: 0; Sodium: 87 mg

Pound Cake

Pound cake is wonderful served plain or topped with a sauce or jam. It is also a good base for fresh fruit desserts such as trifles and fruit fools.

2 ¼ cups all-purpose unbleached flour
¾ teaspoon baking powder
¼ teaspoon baking soda
¼ teaspoon salt
⅛ teaspoon ground mace (optional)
½ cup (1 stick) corn oil margarine
1 cup sugar
3 large egg whites
1½ teaspoons pure vanilla extract
¾ cup buttermilk

1. Preheat the oven to 350°F. Combine the flour, baking powder, baking soda, salt, and mace in a medium-size bowl and mix well. Set aside.

2. In another bowl, cream the margarine and sugar together until smooth. Add the egg whites and vanilla and blend until satin smooth. Alternately add the flour mixture and buttermilk in two additions each, blending well after each addition.

3. Spoon batter into a standard 8½ x 4½-inch loaf pan that has been sprayed with nonstick vegetable spray. Bake until lightly browned and a knife inserted in the center comes out clean, about 1 hour. Remove from the oven and cool on a rack.

MAKES SIXTEEN ½-INCH-SLICE SERVINGS

Each serving contains approximately: Calories: 169; Grams of fat: 6; Cholesterol: negligible; Sodium: 181 mg

Cinnamon Angel Food Cake

The hint of cinnamon in this recipe gives it a slightly different taste than most angel food cakes. However, if you prefer, you can omit it or substitute grated lemon rind or almond extract for more traditional flavor.

1¼ cups sifted cake flour
1¼ cups sugar
½ teaspoon ground cinnamon
12 large egg whites (1 ½ cups)
1½ teaspoons cream of tartar
¼ teaspoon salt
1 teaspoon pure vanilla extract

1. Preheat the oven to 375°F. Have ready but do not grease or spray a 10-inch tube pan. Sift the flour with ¾ cup of the sugar and the cinnamon two times and set aside.

2. Beat the egg whites with the cream of tartar, salt, and vanilla in a very large bowl with an electric mixer until soft, glossy peaks form. Add the remaining ½ cup sugar 2 tablespoons at a time, continuing to beat until the egg whites hold stiff peaks.

3. Sift about one quarter of the flour mixture over the whites and fold in. Repeat, folding in the remaining flour by fourths. Pour batter into the pan and bake until the top is golden brown, 35 to 40 minutes. Remove from the oven and invert in the pan on a rack to cool. Cool completely before removing the cake from the pan.

MAKES ONE 10-INCH CAKE; 16 SERVINGS

Each serving contains approximately: Calories: 104;
Grams of fat: negligible; Cholesterol: 0; Sodium: 100 mg

Hot Milk Cake

This is a recipe I developed for a reader requesting a cake without cane or beet sugar. I used pure crystalline fructose which is sweeter than regular sugar or sucrose, so I was also able to cut back on the amount of it I used.

½ cup nonfat milk
1 tablespoon corn oil margarine
¼ teaspoon salt
4 large egg whites
2 teaspoons canola oil
⅔ cup pure crystalline fructose (available in most supermarkets and
  health food stores)
1 cup all-purpose unbleached flour
1 teaspoon baking powder
1 teaspoon pure vanilla extract

1. Preheat the oven to 350°F. Spray an 8-inch-square baking pan with nonstick vegetable spray.

2. Combine the milk, margarine, and salt, heat until hot but not boiling, and set aside.

3. In a large bowl, beat the egg whites and oil together until blended. Gradually add the fructose and beat until well mixed. Pour in the hot milk and mix well. Add the flour, baking powder, and vanilla and mix well. Pour the batter into the pan and bake until the cake springs back when touched lightly, 25 to 30 minutes.

MAKES 8 SERVINGS

Each serving contains approximately: Calories: 156; Grams of fat: 3;
Cholesterol: negligible; Sodium: 208 mg

Blintz Torte

This recipe is a revision of a reader's favorite dessert recipe. Even though this version only has half the calories of the original, it is still a delicious and unusual cake.

½ cup (1 stick) corn oil margarine
¾ cup plus 1 tablespoon sugar
½ cup nonfat liquid egg substitute
1 teaspoon pure vanilla extract
1¼ cups nonfat milk
3 tablespoons all-purpose unbleached flour
1 teaspoon baking powder
5 large egg whites
⅓ cup chopped almonds
1 teaspoon ground cinnamon

FOR THE CUSTARD FILLING
1 cup nonfat milk
¼ cup sugar
1 tablespoon cornstarch
¼ cup nonfat liquid egg substitute
½ teaspoon pure vanilla extract

1. Combine the margarine and ¼ cup of the sugar and blend until smooth and creamy. Add the egg substitute, vanilla, and milk and mix well.

2. Sift the flour and baking powder together. Gradually beat into the batter. Spread the mixture on the bottom of two 8-inch round cake pans.

3. Beat the egg whites with an electric mixer until they form stiff, dry peaks. Gradually add ½ cup of the sugar and continue beating until well mixed. Spread the egg white mixture over the batter in the cake pans. Sprinkle with the chopped almonds.

4. Mix the remaining tablespoon sugar and the cinnamon together and sprinkle evenly over the top of the egg whites and nuts. Bake until golden brown, about 30 minutes.

5. Meanwhile, make the custard filling. Scald the milk, heating it in a saucepan over medium heat until bubbles form around the edge of the pan. Mix the sugar and cornstarch together. Add to the milk, stirring to blend. Gradually pour the mixture over the egg substitute, stirring constantly. Cook in the top of a double boiler over simmering water, stirring constantly, until thickened. Cool and stir in the vanilla.

6. Cool the cakes. Remove from the pans and spread the filling between the layers. Refrigerate until well chilled before serving.

MAKES ONE 8-INCH CAKE; 12 SERVINGS

Each serving contains approximately: Calories: 210; Grams of fat: 10; Cholesterol: 1 mg; Sodium: 221 mg

Fourth of July Cake

I first saw a cake decorated to look like an American flag many years ago at a Fourth of July picnic and I have never forgotten it. I was so impressed, both by the originality of the idea and the taste of the cake, that I have been working on my own version ever since. I served this cake at my own Independence Day party this year and all of my guests loved it.

⅓ cup corn oil margarine
1½ cups sugar
1 teaspoon pure vanilla extract
2½ cups all-purpose unbleached flour
1½ teaspoons baking soda
1½ teaspoons baking powder
¼ teaspoon salt
1½ cups buttermilk
5 large egg whites, beaten until stiff but not dry peaks form
Creamy Frosting (recipe follows)
¾ cup fresh blueberries, picked over and rinsed
1 cup fresh raspberries

1. Preheat the oven to 350°F. Spray a 9 x 13-inch baking pan with nonstick vegetable spray. Set aside.

2. Cream the margarine and sugar together in a large bowl. Beat in the vanilla. In a medium-size bowl, combine the flour, baking soda, baking powder, and salt and mix well. Add the flour mixture alternately with the buttermilk to the creamed mixture, beating well after each addition. Gently fold in the beaten egg whites.

3. Pour the batter into the prepared pan. Bake until the cake is golden and springs back when lightly touched, about 30 minutes. Cool on a wire rack, then turn out on a serving platter.

4. Frost the cake, reserving about ½ cup of the frosting for decorating with a pastry bag, if desired. To make the cake look like an American flag, turn it so it faces sideways (13 inches across). Make the blue background for stars by placing blueberries in rows in the upper left corner. It will be approximately 9 rows across and 6 rows down, but it depends on the size of the blueberries. Make the 7 red stripes with single rows of raspberries. If using a pastry bag, pipe around the edges of the cake and make dots for the stars. To serve, cut into quarters, both lengthwise and horizontally, making 16 pieces.

MAKES 16 SERVINGS

Each serving contains approximately: Calories: 276; Grams of fat: 10; Cholesterol: 1 mg; Sodium: 163 mg

Creamy Frosting

2½ tablespoons all-purpose unbleached flour
½ cup nonfat milk
½ cup (1 stick) corn oil margarine, at room temperature
⅓ cup sugar
½ teaspoon pure vanilla extract

1. Place the flour in a small saucepan. Add the milk slowly, stirring with a wire whisk until the mixture is smooth and blended.

Cook over medium-low heat, stirring constantly, until thickened, smooth, and fairly stiff. Cool completely.

2. Place the margarine in a small bowl and beat until creamy. Add the sugar gradually and beat until the mixture is light. Add the cooled flour mixture and beat at high speed until light and fluffy, 1 to 2 minutes. Stir in the vanilla.

MAKES 1¼ CUPS (NUTRITIONAL INFORMATION INCLUDED IN THAT FOR THE CAKE)

Coffee Cake

This recipe is a revision of a coffee cake that was literally twice as high in both calories and fat as this one. It is still such a rich cake that it can be served either for a decadent breakfast bread or a very satisfying dessert.

FOR THE CAKE
¼ cup (½ stick) corn oil margarine, at room temperature
¼ cup buttermilk
¾ cup sugar
1 teaspoon pure vanilla extract
1 large egg plus 3 large egg whites
2 cups all-purpose unbleached flour
1 teaspoon baking powder
1 teaspoon baking soda
One 8-ounce container light sour cream

FOR THE FILLING
3 tablespoons corn oil margarine
3 tablespoons buttermilk
¾ cup firmly packed dark brown sugar
2 teaspoons ground cinnamon
½ cup chopped walnuts, toasted in a 350°F oven until golden brown, 8 to 10 minutes

1. Preheat the oven to 350°F. Spray a 10-inch tube pan with nonstick vegetable spray and set aside.

2. To make the cake, combine the margarine, buttermilk, sugar, and vanilla in a large bowl and blend until smooth. Add the egg and egg whites and beat well. In another bowl combine the flour, baking powder, and baking soda, then add it to the creamed mixture alternately with the sour cream, blending well. The batter will be thick.

3. To make the filling, combine the margarine, buttermilk, brown sugar, and cinnamon and blend until smooth. Add the toasted nuts and mix well. Spread half the cake batter in the pan. Dot evenly with half the filling mixture. Cover with the remaining batter and dot with the remaining filling. Bake until a knife inserted in the center of the cake comes out clean, about 50 minutes. Remove the cake from the oven and allow to cool in the pan for 10 minutes. Remove from the pan and finish cooling on a rack.

MAKES ONE 10-INCH CAKE; 12 SERVINGS

Each serving contains approximately: Calories: 443; Grams of fat: 26; Cholesterol: 62 mg; Sodium: 224 mg

Rice Cake

This unusual cake is best topped with fresh or cooked fruit. I particularly like it with cooked figs.

¾ cup long-grain white rice
1½ cups cold water
¼ teaspoon salt
1 cup plus 2 tablespoons nonfat milk
1 cup plus 2 tablespoons hot water
¾ cup plus 2 tablespoons sugar
2 tablespoons unsalted corn oil margarine
Zest of 2 large lemons, finely diced
1 tablespoon all-purpose unbleached flour

¼ cup nonfat liquid egg substitute

2 large egg whites

⅓ cup almonds, toasted in a 350°F oven until golden brown, 8 to 10
minutes, and finely ground

1. Place the rice, cold water, and salt in a 2-quart saucepan.
Cover and bring to a boil over medium heat. Boil for 5 minutes,
drain well, and allow to cool.

2. Heat the milk in a 2-quart saucepan over medium heat.
When steam starts to show, add the hot water, ¾ cup of the sugar,
the margarine, lemon zest, and cooled rice. Cover the saucepan and
bring the mixture to a boil. Uncover the pan and simmer 20 minutes over low heat, stirring frequently until all the liquid is absorbed.

3. Preheat the oven to 350°F. Spray a 9-inch-square baking
pan with nonstick vegetable spray, then dust with the flour, shaking
out any excess. Place a round of parchment or waxed paper in the
bottom of the pan and spray it also.

4. In a small bowl, beat the egg substitute with the remaining
2 tablespoons sugar. In a medium-size bowl, beat the egg whites
with an electric mixer until they hold firm, but not stiff, peaks.
Blend the egg substitute into the whites using a rubber spatula. Fold
in the almonds and 1 tablespoon of the rice mixture. Gently combine this mixture with the remaining rice mixture.

5. Pour the batter into the prepared pan and spread it out
evenly with a rubber spatula. Bake until the cake is set and light
brown, about 30 minutes.

6. Remove from the oven and cool on a wire rack for 15 minutes. Place a plate over the cake pan and gently invert the pan. Lift
off the pan and peel the paper off the back of the cake. Cool the
cake completely. The cake will keep, well covered, in the refrigerator for 3 days.

MAKES ONE 9-INCH CAKE; 12 SERVINGS

*Each serving contains approximately: Calories: 166; Grams of fat: 6.7;
Cholesterol: 1 mg; Sodium: 82 mg*

Lekach (Honey Walnut Cake)

¼ cup (½ stick) corn oil margarine
⅓ cup firmly packed light brown sugar
⅓ cup honey
¼ cup nonfat liquid egg substitute
1 cup all-purpose unbleached flour
1 teaspoon regular or decaffeinated instant coffee granules
¼ teaspoon baking soda
¼ teaspoon ground cinnamon
¼ teaspoon ground allspice
¼ teaspoon ground cloves
½ cup buttermilk
¼ cup walnuts, chopped

1. Preheat the oven to 350°F. Combine the margarine, brown sugar, and honey and blend until creamy in a large bowl. Beat in the egg substitute. Add the remaining ingredients and mix well.

2. Pour into an 8-inch-square baking pan sprayed with non-stick vegetable spray. Bake until a knife inserted in the center of the cake comes out clean, 20 to 25 minutes. Cool in the pan on a wire rack before serving.

MAKES ONE 8-INCH CAKE; 9 SERVINGS

Each serving contains approximately: Calories: 179; Grams of fat: 7.6; Cholesterol: 1 mg; Sodium: 55 mg

Applesauce Cake

In this recipe I have used dried rather than the candied fruit more usually found in this type of cake. I think it gives it a lighter, cleaner taste.

1⅓ cups sugar
½ cup (1 stick) corn oil margarine

From the bottom, counterclockwise: Fourth of July Cake (page 117), Apple Upside-Down Cake (page 125), and Prune and Pecan Bundt Cake (page 128).

From the top: Peanut Clusters (page 233), Chocolate Bagels (page 180), Almond Macaroons (page 173), Cinnamon Sticks (page 175), and Walnut Biscotti (page 174).

From the top: Strawberry Napoleon (page 21), Fruit Gazpacho (page 6), and Fantasy in Fruit (page 8).

From the top left: Vanilla Pots de Crème (page 26), Year Around Summer
Pudding (page 50), Peach Melba Trifle (page 42), and Vanilla Yogurt
Terrine with Fruit Coulis (page 30).

From the left: Sugar-Free Apple Strudel (page 105), Spiced Pear Turnovers (page 104), and Fruit Pizza (page 108).

From the top: Fire and Ice (page 220), Cranberry Bars (page 167), and Neapolitan Bombe (page 222).

From the top: Chocolate Crepes with Cinnamon-Apple Filling and Vanilla Cream Spread (page 191), Cinnamon Crispas (page 198), and Soufflé-Filled Crepes (page 194).

From the top: Strawberry Mousse with Raspberry Sauce (page 56), Grand Marnier Soufflé (page 66), and Orange Mousse (page 60).

½ cup buttermilk

2 cups unsweetened applesauce

½ cup nonfat liquid egg substitute

1 tablespoon hot water

3½ cups all-purpose unbleached flour

2½ teaspoons baking soda

1 teaspoon ground cloves

1 teaspoon freshly grated nutmeg

1 teaspoon ground cinnamon

⅓ cup dark raisins

½ cup pecans, chopped and toasted in a 350°F oven until golden
    brown, 8 to 10 minutes

⅓ cup dried cherries

⅓ cup chopped dried dates

½ cup chopped dried pineapple

1. Preheat the oven to 325°F. Spray a 10-inch tube pan with nonstick vegetable spray and set aside. Cream the sugar and margarine together until smooth. Add the buttermilk, applesauce, egg substitute, and hot water and mix well.

2. Sift the flour, baking soda, and spices together three times, then add it to the creamed mixture. Add the raisins, pecans, cherries, dates, and pineapple. Mix well and pour into the pan. Bake until a knife inserted into the center of the cake comes out clean, about 1 hour and 20 minutes. Remove from the oven and cool completely before removing from the pan.

MAKES ONE 10-INCH CAKE; 16 SERVINGS

*Each serving contains approximately: Calories: 318; Grams of fat: 9;
Cholesterol: negligible; Sodium: 213 mg*

Apple Snackin' Cake

This is a recipe I developed for an Autumn Picnic menu for *Cooking Light* magazine and it is still one of my favorite portable desserts. Lining the baking pan with foil makes it easy to lift the cooled cake out of the pan and wrap it up. It also makes cleaning the pan very easy!

2 tablespoons corn oil margarine
⅓ cup sugar
2 large egg whites
⅓ cup nonfat milk
⅓ cup unsweetened applesauce
1 teaspoon vanilla butter and nut flavoring (look for it where the extracts are sold in the supermarket)
1⅓ cups all-purpose unbleached flour
2 teaspoons baking powder
¼ teaspoon salt
2 large Golden Delicious apples (1 pound), peeled, cored, and thinly sliced

FOR THE TOPPING

3 tablespoons sugar
1 teaspoon ground cinnamon
3 tablespoons all-purpose unbleached flour
1 tablespoon corn oil margarine

1. Preheat the oven to 350°F. Line a 9-inch-square pan with aluminum foil, allowing enough overhang (about 6 inches on each side) so that the cake can be removed from the pan and wrapped after being baked and cooled. Spray the foil liner with nonstick vegetable spray and set aside.

2. Combine the margarine and sugar in a medium-size bowl and mix until creamy and smooth. Add the egg whites and mix well. Add the milk, applesauce, and flavoring and mix well.

3. In a large bowl, combine the flour, baking powder, and salt. Add the liquid ingredients to the dry ingredients and stir just until

the dry ingredients are moistened. Do not overmix. Spread the batter into the foil-lined pan and press the apple slices down into the batter, covering the batter with about 3 rows of apple slices.

4. To make the topping, combine the sugar, cinnamon, and flour and mix well. Add the margarine and mix just until it has the consistency of coarse gravel. Sprinkle the topping evenly over the apples and bake until the top is golden brown, 45 to 50 minutes. Place on a rack and allow to cool to room temperature before wrapping the cake in the foil liner.

MAKES ONE 9-INCH CAKE; 12 SERVINGS

Each serving contains approximately: Calories: 153; Grams of fat: 3.2;
Cholesterol: negligible; Sodium: 122 mg

Apple Upside-Down Cake

Most people automatically think of pineapple for an old-fashioned upside-down cake, but apples offer a deliciously different taste and texture. I prefer to use Golden Delicious apples for this cake because they are so sweet and hold their texture well.

¼ cup chopped walnuts, plus 1 walnut half
2 tablespoons corn oil margarine
3 tablespoons firmly packed dark brown sugar
One 12-ounce can frozen unsweetened apple juice concentrate, thawed
3 large Golden Delicious apples, peeled, cored, and sliced into ¼-inch
  rings
1½ cups all-purpose unbleached flour
1 tablespoon baking powder
1 tablespoon ground cinnamon
½ teaspoon salt
3 large egg whites
¼ cup canola or corn oil
1 tablespoon pure vanilla extract

1. Preheat the oven to 350°F. Place the walnuts on a baking sheet and toast in the oven until golden brown, 8 to 10 minutes. Watch carefully because they burn easily. Set aside.

2. In a heavy 10-inch skillet melt the margarine over low heat. Add the brown sugar and ¼ cup of the apple juice concentrate, bring to a boil over low heat, and simmer, stirring constantly, for 2 minutes. Remove from the heat.

3. Place one apple ring in the center of the skillet. Cut the remaining apple rings in half and arrange them around it in a spoke pattern. Place the walnut half in the center of the apple ring and set the skillet aside.

4. Combine the flour, baking powder, cinnamon, and salt in a bowl and mix well. In a large bowl, using an electric mixer, beat the egg whites until soft peaks form. Continue beating while adding the remaining apple juice concentrate, the oil, and vanilla. Slowly beat in the dry ingredients. When well mixed, fold in the toasted walnuts and carefully spoon the batter over the apples in the skillet. Bake in the center of the oven until golden brown and a knife inserted in the center of the cake comes out clean, about 50 minutes. Cool on a wire rack for 15 minutes before turning upside down onto a serving plate. (Some of the apples may stick to the skillet. Just remove them with a spatula and place them back on top of the cake.)

MAKES ONE 10-INCH CAKE; 16 SERVINGS

Each serving contains approximately: Calories: 138; Grams of fat: 6.3; Cholesterol: 0; Sodium: 152 mg

Apple Crumb Cake

This recipe is one of those revisions where the only thing I could preserve from the original recipe was the basic taste. My reader's recipe called for 1½ cups of butter, which made a very moist cake. To achieve this almost pudding texture without all of the fat, I have used 1½ cups of applesauce and only 3 tablespoons of corn oil margarine. For a bit sweeter cake, you can use Golden Delicious apples rather than the apples called for in the recipe.

1½ cups plus 3 tablespoons all-purpose unbleached flour
1 teaspoon baking powder
½ teaspoon baking soda
1 large egg
1 teaspoon pure vanilla extract
¼ cup light corn syrup
3 tablespoons corn oil margarine, melted
1½ cups unsweetened applesauce
1½ pounds (4 medium-size) McIntosh or Rome Beauty apples,
* peeled, cored, and thinly sliced*
¼ cup sugar
1 teaspoon ground cinnamon
2 tablespoons corn oil margarine

1. Preheat the oven to 350°F. Combine all but 3 tablespoons of the flour, the baking powder, and baking soda in a large bowl and mix well. Add the egg, vanilla, corn syrup, melted margarine, and applesauce and mix just until moistened. Spread in a 9 x 13-inch baking dish sprayed with nonstick vegetable spray. Layer the apple slices over the top.

2. Combine the remaining 3 tablespoons of flour with the sugar and cinnamon and mix well. Mix in the margarine with a pastry blender or fork until crumbs form. (Some crumbs may be large, others small.) Sprinkle the mixture evenly over the apples and bake until the apples are soft and a knife inserted in the center comes out clean, about 35 minutes.

MAKES 16 SERVINGS

Each serving contains approximately: Calories: 137; Grams of fat: 4;
Cholesterol: 13 mg; Sodium: 118 mg

Prune and Pecan Bundt Cake

I have always liked to make Bundt cakes because their fluted pattern makes them so pretty that they really don't need any other decoration. However, the glaze on this cake does give it a lovely "finished" look. The prunes help to keep the cake moist as well as adding a rich and delicious flavor.

1⅓ cups chopped pitted dried prunes (about 26 prunes)
1 cup buttermilk
2 cups all-purpose unbleached flour
1 teaspoon baking soda
1½ teaspoons ground cinnamon
1 teaspoon freshly grated nutmeg
½ teaspoon ground allspice
¼ teaspoon salt
⅓ cup granulated sugar
⅓ cup firmly packed dark brown sugar
¼ cup canola oil
2 teaspoons pure vanilla extract
1 large egg plus 3 large egg whites, lightly beaten
2 tablespoons finely chopped pecans

FOR THE GLAZE

½ cup sugar
½ cup buttermilk
½ teaspoon baking soda
2 tablespoons corn oil margarine

1. Preheat the oven to 350°F. Combine half of the chopped prunes and ½ cup of the buttermilk in a blender or food processor and puree. Pour in a large bowl. Add the remaining chopped prunes and buttermilk, mix well, and set aside.

2. In another large bowl, combine the flour, baking soda, spices, salt, and both sugars and mix well.

3. Add the oil, vanilla, and eggs to the prune-buttermilk mixture and mix well. Pour the liquid ingredients into the dry ingredients and stir until thoroughly mixed.

4. Spoon batter into a 9-inch (12-cup) Bundt pan sprayed with nonstick vegetable coating and bake in the center of the oven until the cake pulls away from the sides of the pan and is springy to the touch, 40 to 45 minutes. Cool the cake upright in the pan on a wire rack for 15 minutes.

5. While cake is cooling, place the chopped pecans in a pie plate or on an ungreased baking sheet and toast in the oven until golden brown, 8 to 10 minutes. Watch carefully, as they burn easily. Set aside.

6. When cooled, loosen the cake all around the edges with a thin-bladed spatula. Invert onto a rack and pierce the cake all over with a fork.

7. Combine the glaze ingredients in a saucepan and cook over medium heat, stirring constantly, until the margarine melts and the mixture boils. Immediately remove from the heat and slowly ladle the buttermilk glaze evenly over the cooled cake. (Only about half the glaze will adhere to the cake.) Immediately sprinkle with the toasted pecans and transfer to a serving platter to slice.

MAKES ONE 9-INCH CAKE; 16 SERVINGS

Each serving contains approximately: Calories: 209; Grams of fat: 6.2; Cholesterol: 14 mg; Sodium: 155 mg

Gingerbread

I have always been extremely fond of gingerbread and this recipe is especially good because of the addition of the crystallized ginger which can be found in the Asian section of most supermarkets. It adds to the flavor and also to the texture. I like to top each serving with a dollop of low-fat whipped topping or a little vanilla ice milk or nonfat frozen yogurt.

¼ cup (½ stick) corn oil margarine, melted and cooled
⅓ cup firmly packed dark brown sugar
¼ cup nonfat liquid egg substitute
¼ cup buttermilk
2 cups all-purpose unbleached flour
1½ teaspoons baking soda
1 teaspoon ground cinnamon
1 teaspoon ground ginger
1 teaspoon minced crystallized ginger
½ teaspoon salt
½ cup golden molasses
¼ cup honey
1 cup hot water
Light whipped topping (optional)

1. Preheat the oven to 350°F. Combine the margarine, brown sugar, egg substitute, and buttermilk in a large bowl and set aside.

2. In a medium-size bowl, combine the flour, baking soda, cinnamon, both gingers, and salt. In a 2-cup measuring cup or small bowl, stir together the molasses, honey, and hot water. Using a wire whisk, add the flour mixture alternately with the molasses mixture to the margarine mixture, adding half the ingredients at a time. Stir until most lumps are gone, but do not overbeat.

3. Pour the batter into a 9-inch-square or 11 x 7-inch baking pan sprayed with nonstick vegetable spray. Bake until a knife inserted in the center of the cake comes out clean, 40 to 45 minutes. Top with whipped topping, if desired.

MAKES 8 SERVINGS

Each serving contains approximately: Calories: 236; Grams of fat: 6.3; Cholesterol: negligible; Sodium: 348 mg

NOTE: This is a moist but light cake with just the right amount of ginger. The whipped topping, even used sparingly, complements it perfectly.

Strawberry Cake

This pretty pink cake is perfect for bridal showers—or anytime you want a tasty, pastel cake for your party. When fresh strawberries are in season, they make an attractive decoration and whole strawberries can be used for candle holders if you are serving this cake for a birthday party.

One 18½-ounce box light white cake mix
One 16-ounce bag frozen unsweetened strawberries, thawed, mashed, and drained, reserving 2 tablespoons of the juice
½ cup water
3 large egg whites
1 teaspoon pure strawberry extract
½ cup confectioners' sugar

1. Preheat the oven to 350°F. Spray a 9 x 13-inch glass baking dish with nonstick vegetable spray.

2. Place the cake mix in a large bowl and add the strawberries, water, egg whites, and extract. Blend on low speed with an electric mixer for 30 seconds. Beat on medium speed 2 minutes, scraping the sides of the bowl with a rubber spatula. Pour into the pan.

3. Bake until the top springs back when touched lightly, about 30 minutes. Combine the reserved strawberry juice with the confectioners' sugar and pour evenly over the warm cake.

MAKES 12 SERVINGS

Each serving contains approximately: Calories: 218; Grams of fat: 3; Cholesterol: 0; Sodium: 340 mg

Strawberry Shortcake

You see so many recipes for strawberry shortcake that call for angel food cake, pound cake, or just plain white cake. My favorite is still the old-fashioned version made with biscuits and served while they are still warm. However, I do like to sweeten the strawberries with a little orange marmalade, which gives them a different taste that I like very much.

FOR THE STRAWBERRY FILLING

2 pints fresh strawberries, hulled and sliced
1 tablespoon sugar
2 tablespoons fruit-sweetened orange marmalade or other flavor jam

FOR THE SHORTCAKE

1¾ cups all-purpose unbleached flour
2 tablespoons sugar
1 tablespoon baking powder
¼ teaspoon salt
3 tablespoons corn oil margarine
½ cup plus 2 tablespoons nonfat milk
Light whipped topping

1. Combine the strawberries, sugar, and marmalade. Allow to stand at room temperature for about 1 hour while you make the shortcake.

2. Preheat the oven to 450°F. In a large bowl, combine the flour, sugar, baking powder, and salt. Cut the margarine into the flour mixture until it resembles coarse crumbs. Add the milk and stir gently until the mixture forms a mass. Gather it into a ball.

3. Transfer the dough to a lightly floured surface. Knead it for 30 seconds, then pat it out to a ¾-inch-thick rectangle. Using a 3-inch biscuit cutter, cut 8 circles, using up all the dough.

4. Arrange the biscuits 1 inch apart on an ungreased baking sheet. Bake until puffed and golden, 8 to 10 minutes. Allow the biscuits to cool on a wire rack.

5. Just before serving, halve the biscuits and place the bottom halves on serving plates. Cover each with ¼ cup of the filling. Place the tops on and cover with another 2 tablespoons of the filling. If desired, top each serving with whipped topping.

MAKES 8 SERVINGS

Each serving contains approximately: Calories: 125; Grams of fat: 3.2; Cholesterol: negligible; Sodium: 144

Cranberry Sauce Cake

Using a reduced-fat mayonnaise and toasting the walnuts to enhance their flavor so that I could use fewer of them made it possible for me to revise this unusual holiday cake without losing the uniqueness of its taste and texture.

One 16-ounce can whole cranberry sauce
¾ cup reduced-fat mayonnaise
1 tablespoon grated orange rind
⅓ cup frozen unsweetened orange juice concentrate, thawed
½ cup walnuts, chopped and toasted in a 350°F oven until golden brown, 8 to 10 minutes
3 cups all-purpose unbleached flour
1¼ cups sugar
1 teaspoon baking soda
½ teaspoon salt

Preheat the oven to 350°F. Spray a standard-size Bundt or tube pan with nonstick vegetable spray. Mix all the ingredients together well in a large bowl and pour into the pan. Bake until a knife inserted in the center of the cake comes out clean, 55 to 60 minutes.

MAKES 16 SERVINGS

Each serving contains approximately: Calories: 252; Grams of fat: 6; Cholesterol: 4 mg; Sodium: 202 mg

Peach Kuchen

1 cup all-purpose unbleached flour
½ teaspoon baking powder
¼ teaspoon salt
2 teaspoons ground cinnamon
½ cup firmly packed dark brown sugar
¼ cup (½ stick) corn oil margarine
12 fresh peach halves, peeled
¼ cup nonfat liquid egg substitute
1 cup canned evaporated skim milk
1 teaspoon pure vanilla extract

1. Preheat the oven to 400°F. Sift together the flour, baking powder, salt, 1 teaspoon of the cinnamon, and 2 tablespoons of the sugar. Cut in the margarine using two 2 knives or a pastry blender until the mixture looks like cornmeal.

2. Spoon into an 8-inch-square pan sprayed with nonstick vegetable spray and pat an even layer of the crumb mixture over the bottom and halfway up the sides of the pan. Place the peaches on top of the pastry. Combine the remaining sugar with the remaining 1 teaspoon of cinnamon and sprinkle over the peaches. Bake for 15 minutes.

3. Combine the egg substitute, evaporated milk, and vanilla in a small bowl. Pour over the baked mixture and bake until the liquid is absorbed, about 30 minutes longer.

MAKES ONE 8-INCH CAKE; 9 SERVINGS

Each serving contains approximately: Calories: 190; Grams of fat: 6; Cholesterol: 1 mg; Sodium: 199 mg

Light Lemon Cake

Lemon is a very popular flavor because it goes well with so many other flavors. I particularly like this cake with fresh berries. I fill the center of it with the berries and then serve a few of them on the side with each slice of cake.

⅓ cup (⅔ stick) corn oil margarine
1 cup sugar
¾ cup nonfat liquid egg substitute
2½ cups cake flour
3 teaspoons baking powder
½ teaspoon baking soda
½ teaspoon salt
1 cup buttermilk
1½ teaspoons pure vanilla extract
2 teaspoons grated lemon rind
2 teaspoons fresh lemon juice

1. Preheat the oven to 325°F. Combine the margarine with the sugar in a large bowl and blend until light and fluffy. Add the egg substitute and mix well.

2. Sift together the flour, baking powder, baking soda, and salt in a medium-size bowl, then resift three more times. Add the sifted ingredients to the margarine mixture in thirds, alternating with the buttermilk. Beat the batter thoroughly after each addition. Add the vanilla, lemon rind, and lemon juice and beat 2 minutes. Pour the batter into a standard-size Bundt pan sprayed well with nonstick vegetable coating. Bake until a knife inserted in the center of the cake comes out clean, about 55 minutes.

MAKES 16 SERVINGS

Each serving contains approximately: Calories: 157; Grams of fat: 5; Cholesterol: 1 mg; Sodium: 271 mg

Lemon Meringue Spiral

This is a rather complicated recipe, but well worth the time it takes to make it. It can be served right out of the oven, but I think it is better served cold.

1 large egg plus 3 large egg whites
⅓ cup sugar
1 teaspoon pure vanilla extract
⅔ cup all-purpose unbleached flour
1 teaspoon baking powder
⅛ teaspoon salt
Grated rind of 1 lemon
1 tablespoon confectioners' sugar, sifted

FOR THE LEMON FILLING
½ cup sugar
⅛ teaspoon salt
5 tablespoons cornstarch
1½ cups boiling water
⅓ cup nonfat liquid egg substitute
2 tablespoons grated lemon rind
½ cup fresh lemon juice

FOR THE MERINGUE
5 large egg whites
¼ teaspoon cream of tartar
½ cup sugar

1. Preheat the oven to 375°F. Spray a 15 ½ x 10 ½ x 1-inch jelly-roll pan with nonstick vegetable spray. Line with waxed paper, leaving a 2-inch overhang, then spray and flour the paper.

2. To make the cake, in a large bowl beat the egg and egg whites, sugar, and vanilla until very thick and pale, about 5 minutes. Fold in the flour, baking powder, salt, and lemon rind. Spread the mixture evenly in the lined pan and bake until lightly brown and the center springs back when lightly pressed, about 8 minutes.

3. Sprinkle the top with the confectioners' sugar. Cover with a towel and invert onto a wire rack. Remove the pan and peel off the paper. Roll up the cake and towel together from a narrow end. Place the roll seam side down on the wire rack. Cool to room temperature.

4. To make the filling, combine the sugar, salt, and cornstarch in a saucepan. Stir in the boiling water and continue to stir over medium heat until the mixture boils, thickens, and clears. Pour the egg substitute in a bowl and stir in a little of the hot mixture. Pour into the saucepan and stir. Stir in the lemon rind and juice. Cook 2 minutes, stirring constantly. Remove from the heat and cool to room temperature. Cover the surface of the filling with plastic wrap (this will prevent a skin from forming) and refrigerate until chilled.

5. To make the meringue, beat the egg whites and cream of tartar with an electric mixer until soft peaks form. Slowly beat in the sugar until stiff peaks form. Set aside.

6. Preheat the oven to 400°F. Unroll the cake onto an oven-proof platter. Spread with the filling, leaving a 1-inch border. Roll the cake up tightly and place seam side down. Spread a ½-inch-thick layer of meringue smoothly over the roll. If desired, pipe the remaining meringue over the roll, otherwise, spread the remaining meringue decoratively over the roll. Bake until the peaks are golden brown, 5 to 8 minutes. Cut into 8 pieces and serve hot or chilled.

MAKES 8 SERVINGS

Each serving contains approximately: Calories: 237; Grams of fat: 1; Cholesterol: 27 mg; Sodium: 242 mg

Citrus Pudding Cake

Just as the name indicates, this is a moist, heavy, almost pudding-textured cake. It is wonderful served with sliced fresh fruit. In fact, I often omit the icing and top each slice with fresh berries when I serve it.

One 18½-ounce box light white cake mix
1 cup nonfat plain yogurt
2 tablespoons grated orange rind
½ cup fresh orange juice
1 large egg
2 large egg whites
½ cup water
2 tablespoons canola oil
1 teaspoon pure vanilla extract

FOR THE ICING

½ cup sifted confectioners' sugar
1 tablespoon fresh lemon juice
¼ teaspoon pure vanilla extract

1. Preheat the oven to 350°F. Spray a standard–size Bundt pan with nonstick vegetable spray and set aside.

2. Combine the cake mix, yogurt, orange rind, orange juice, egg and egg whites, water, oil, and vanilla in a large bowl. Using an electric mixer, beat on low speed for 4 minutes. Pour the batter into the Bundt pan and bake until a knife inserted in the center of the cake comes out clean, about 50 minutes. Cool on a wire rack for 10 minutes, then turn out onto a serving plate and allow to cool completely.

3. While the cake is cooling, make the icing. Combine the icing ingredients in a bowl and mix well. When the cake is cool, drizzle the icing evenly over the top.

MAKES 12 SERVINGS

Each serving contains approximately: Calories: 237; Grams of fat: 4.7; Cholesterol: 18 mg; Sodium: 328 mg

Apricot Pound Cake

The apricots in this recipe make for an unusual variation on the more usual plain pound cake. I like to thinly slice this cake and then lightly toast it for a teatime "cookie."

1 tablespoon brandy
⅓ cup chopped dried apricots
2¼ cups all-purpose unbleached flour
¾ teaspoon baking powder
¼ teaspoon baking soda
¼ teaspoon salt
½ cup (1 stick) corn oil margarine
1 cup sugar
3 large egg whites
1½ teaspoons pure vanilla extract
2 teaspoons finely grated orange rind
¾ cup buttermilk

1. Preheat the oven to 350°F. Spray a 9 x 5-inch loaf pan with nonstick vegetable spray. Combine the brandy and apricots in a small bowl and set aside.

2. In a medium-size bowl, combine the flour, baking powder, baking soda, and salt. In another bowl, cream together the margarine and sugar until smooth. Add the egg whites, vanilla, and orange rind and blend until satin smooth. Alternately add the flour and buttermilk to the margarine mixture in two additions each, blending well after each addition.

3. Pour the batter into the pan and bake until a knife inserted in the center of the cake comes out clean, about 1 hour. Cool in the pan for 10 minutes, then remove from the pan and cool on a wire rack until room temperature before slicing.

MAKES 16 THIN SLICES OF CAKE

Each slice contains approximately: Calories: 178; Grams of fat: 6;
Cholesterol: negligible; Sodium: 171 mg

Banana Cake

¾ cup sugar
1 tablespoon corn oil margarine
⅓ cup unsweetened applesauce
3 very ripe bananas, peeled and mashed (about 1 cup)
1 large egg plus 1 large egg white
½ teaspoon pure vanilla extract
1¾ cups cake flour
¼ teaspoon salt
1 teaspoon baking soda

1. Preheat the oven to 350°F. In a medium-size bowl, combine the sugar, margarine, and applesauce and blend until smooth. Blend in the bananas, egg and egg white, and vanilla.

2. Sift the flour, salt, and baking soda together three times. Fold into the banana mixture until just combined. Pour the batter into a 9 x 5-inch loaf pan sprayed with nonstick vegetable spray. Bake until a knife inserted in the center of the cake comes out clean, about 55 minutes. Immediately turn out onto a wire rack to cool.

MAKES 16 SLICES

Each slice contains approximately: Calories: 110; Grams of fat: 1; Cholesterol: 13 mg; Sodium: 105 mg

Hummingbird Cake

I have never quite been able to figure out why this combination of ingredients was named hummingbird cake. It seems to me that this hearty, rather heavy cake with a brandy sauce might more appropriately be called "eagle" cake. However, by any name, this is truly a luscious-tasting, satisfying dessert.

3 cups all-purpose unbleached flour

1⅓ cups sugar

½ teaspoon salt

1 teaspoon baking soda

1 teaspoon ground cinnamon

2 large egg yolks

¾ cup canola oil

1½ teaspoons pure vanilla extract

1 cup canned or fresh unsweetened crushed pineapple with natural juice

2 large bananas, peeled and chopped (2 cups)

¾ cup pecans, chopped and toasted in a 350°F oven until golden
    brown, 8 to 10 minutes

3 large egg whites

⅛ teaspoon cream of tartar

Brandy Sauce (recipe follows; optional)

1. Preheat the oven to 350°F. Spray a 10-inch tube pan with nonstick vegetable spray. In a large bowl, sift together the flour, sugar, salt, baking soda, and cinnamon. Make a well in the center and put in the yolks, oil, vanilla, and pineapple. Mix well, but do not beat. The batter will be thick. Fold in the bananas and pecans.

2. In another bowl, beat the egg whites with the cream of tartar with an electric mixer until very stiff peaks form. Fold into the batter and pour into the pan. Bake until a knife inserted in the center of the cake comes out clean, about 1 hour. Cool in the pan for 20 minutes, then invert onto a rack to cool completely. If desired, top with the brandy sauce.

MAKES ONE 10-INCH CAKE; 16 SERVINGS

*Each serving (cake only) contains approximately: Calories: 313;
Grams of fat: 15; Cholesterol: 27 mg; Sodium: 137 mg*

Brandy Sauce

1¼ cups low-fat milk
4 teaspoons cornstarch
2 tablespoons corn oil margarine
½ cup firmly packed dark brown sugar
2 tablespoons brandy or 1 teaspoon pure brandy extract

Combine the milk and cornstarch in a small saucepan and stir until the cornstarch is completely dissolved. Add the margarine and brown sugar and cook over medium heat, stirring constantly with a wire whisk, until the mixture thickens and comes to a boil. Continue to boil for 1 minute. Remove from the heat and stir in the brandy. Serve warm.

MAKES 1 CUP; SIXTEEN 1-TABLESPOON SERVINGS

Each serving contains approximately: Calories: 51; Grams of fat: 2; Cholesterol: 1 mg; Sodium: 31 mg

Fruit Cocktail Cake

This recipe is a makeover of one of my readers' recipes that she said was always a favorite with her church potluck dinners. It is a very moist cake and goes well with almost any kind of menu.

FOR THE CAKE
2 cups all-purpose unbleached flour
3 large egg whites
2 teaspoons baking soda
One 16-ounce can fruit cocktail packed in natural juice, drained
1¼ cups sugar

FOR THE TOPPING
¼ cup (½ stick) corn oil margarine
¾ cup sugar
½ cup buttermilk
1 teaspoon pure vanilla extract

1. Preheat the oven to 350°F. Combine all the cake ingredients in a large bowl and mix well. Spread in a 9 x 13-inch baking pan sprayed with nonstick vegetable spray. Bake until the center springs back when lightly touched, 40 to 45 minutes.

2. While the cake is baking, make the topping. Combine the topping ingredients in a small saucepan. Bring to a full boil, stirring constantly, then take off the heat and set aside.

3. When the cake is done, poke holes all over the top of the cake with a large meat fork. Pour the topping over the cake, tipping the pan if necessary to distribute the topping evenly.

MAKES 16 SERVINGS

Each serving contains approximately: Calories: 194; Grams of fat: 3; Cholesterol: negligible; Sodium: 156 mg

Coffee Rhubarb Cake

⅓ cup (⅔ stick) corn oil margarine
1¼ cups sugar
2 large egg whites
1 cup buttermilk
1½ teaspoons pure vanilla extract
1 teaspoon baking soda
½ cup hot coffee
2 cups all-purpose unbleached flour
¼ teaspoon salt
1½ large stalks rhubarb, diced (2 cups)
1 teaspoon ground cinnamon

1. Preheat the oven to 350°F. Combine the margarine and 1 cup plus 2 tablespoons of the sugar and blend until smooth. Add the egg whites, buttermilk, and vanilla and mix well. Dissolve the baking soda in 2 tablespoons of the hot coffee and stir it into the buttermilk mixture.

2. Combine the flour and salt and stir it into the wet ingredients. Fold in the diced rhubarb and pour the batter into a 9 x 13-inch baking pan sprayed with nonstick vegetable spray. Combine the remaining 2 tablespoons sugar and the cinnamon and sprinkle over the batter.

3. Bake until golden brown, 35 to 40 minutes. Remove from the oven and brush the top of the hot cake with the remaining hot coffee.

MAKES 15 SERVINGS

Each serving contains approximately: Calories: 173; Grams of fat: 4; Cholesterol: 1 mg; Sodium: 175 mg

Zucchini Spice Cake

This recipe is a revision I did for one of my readers several years ago. Since that time I have received so many similar recipes that I decided to include this one in this book.

1½ cups all-purpose unbleached flour
1 teaspoon baking soda
1 teaspoon ground cinnamon
½ teaspoon ground cloves
½ teaspoon freshly grated nutmeg
½ teaspoon ground allspice
¼ teaspoon salt
¾ cup sugar
3 tablespoons canola oil
1 tablespoon white vinegar
1 teaspoon pure vanilla extract
2 cups water
1 small zucchini, grated (½ cup)
¼ cup chopped walnuts, toasted in a 350°F oven until golden brown, 8 to 10 minutes

1. Preheat the oven to 350°F. Spray an 8-inch-square baking pan with nonstick vegetable spray. Set aside.

2. In a large bowl, combine the flour, baking soda, spices, salt, and sugar. In another bowl, combine the oil, vinegar, vanilla, and water. Add the liquid to the dry ingredients and mix until just moistened. Fold in the zucchini and nuts. Spoon the batter into the prepared pan.

3. Bake until a knife inserted in the center of the cake comes out clean, about 1 hour. Cool completely on a wire rack before cutting.

MAKES ONE 8-INCH CAKE; 9 SERVINGS

Each serving contains approximately: Calories: 207; Grams of fat: 6.8; Cholesterol: 0; Sodium: 160 mg

14-Karat Cake

This is a recipe that I developed years ago for one of my sons' fourteenth birthday party. It was such a hit that I increased the amount of carrots from 14 to 18 ounces for his eighteenth birthday and, of course, called it 18-karat cake!

1 cup whole-wheat flour
¼ cup sugar
1 teaspoon baking powder
¾ teaspoon baking soda
¼ teaspoon salt
1 teaspoon ground cinnamon
¼ cup corn oil
2 large eggs, lightly beaten, or ½ cup liquid egg substitute
14 ounces (1¼ cups) grated carrots (3 medium-size carrots)
1 teaspoon grated orange rind
1 large or 2 small oranges, peeled, seeded, and very finely chopped
¼ cup chopped walnuts

1. Preheat the oven to 350°F. Spray an 8½-inch-square cake pan with nonstick vegetable spray. Cut waxed paper to fit the bottom of the pan. (If using a Teflon pan, put waxed paper on the bottom of the pan but do not spray the sides.)

2. Combine the flour, sugar, baking powder, baking soda, salt, and cinnamon in a large bowl. In another bowl, combine the oil and eggs and mix well. Add the liquid ingredients to the dry ingredients and mix well. Add the remaining ingredients and mix well.

3. Pour the batter into the cake pan and bake until a knife inserted in the center of the cake comes out clean, about 35 minutes. Cool on a wire rack for 10 minutes, then remove the cake from the pan and carefully peel off the waxed paper. Cool to room temperature and cover the cake until ready to serve so it will not dry out. If you are keeping the cake for more than a day, I suggest storing it in the refrigerator to preserve freshness.

MAKES ONE 8½-INCH CAKE; 16 SERVINGS

Hawaiian Carrot Cake:

Omit the oranges and grated orange rind and in their place add one 20-ounce can crushed pineapple packed in natural juice, drained. Use only 1 cup of grated carrots instead of 1¾ cups. Follow the directions exactly. Differences in exchanges and calories are negligible.

Each serving contains approximately: Calories: 105; Grams of fat: 5.4; Cholesterol: 27 mg; Sodium: 111 mg

Pumpkin-Pie Cake

A pumpkin dessert is always a popular choice for Halloween and holiday parties. This unusual and delicious cake is sure to please your guests any time of the year and it is a perfect party dessert because it makes so many servings.

One 18½-ounce box light white cake mix
¼ cup (½ stick) corn oil margarine, melted
2 large egg whites
1¼ cups canned evaporated skim milk
4 teaspoons ground cinnamon
2 teaspoons freshly grated nutmeg
One 14-ounce can solid pack pumpkin
1 cup nonfat liquid egg substitute
1¼ cups plus 2 tablespoons sugar
½ teaspoon salt
1 teaspoon ground ginger
½ teaspoon ground cloves
2 tablespoons cold corn oil margarine

1. Preheat the oven to 350°F. Measure out 1 cup of the cake mix and set aside. Combine the remaining mix with the melted margarine, egg whites, ¼ cup of the milk, and 1 teaspoon each of the cinnamon and nutmeg. Mix well and pour into a 10-inch springform pan sprayed with nonstick vegetable spray.

2. In a large bowl, combine the pumpkin with the egg substitute, 1¼ cups of the sugar, 2 teaspoons of the cinnamon, the remaining 1 teaspoon nutmeg, the salt, ginger, cloves, and remaining 1 cup of milk. Mix well with a whisk and pour over the unbaked crust.

3. Combine the reserved 1 cup of cake mix with the remaining 1 teaspoon of cinnamon, the remaining 2 tablespoons of sugar, and the cold margarine. Mix until crumbly and sprinkle over the pumpkin filling. Bake until a knife inserted in the center of the cake comes out clean, about 1½ hours.

MAKES ONE 10-INCH CAKE; 16 SERVINGS

Each serving contains approximately: Calories: 285; Grams of fat: 8;
Cholesterol: 1 mg; Sodium: 410 mg

Chocolate Meringue Cake
with Raspberry Sauce

This is an unusual and deceptively rich-tasting cake. The original recipe that I revised for my column called for a whipped cream topping on the cake. I personally prefer it with just the raspberry sauce. However, it is also wonderful served with vanilla nonfat frozen yogurt.

4 large egg whites
2 teaspoons fresh lemon juice
1½ cups sugar
2 tablespoons corn oil margarine, melted
½ cup unsweetened cocoa powder, sifted
1 cup nonfat milk, at the boiling point
1 teaspoon instant coffee granules
1 teaspoon pure vanilla extract
One 12-ounce bag quick-frozen unsweetened raspberries, thawed
  (2 cups)
Candy coffee beans for garnish (optional)
Fresh mint sprigs for garnish (optional)

1. Preheat the oven to 200°F. Cover two cookie sheets with parchment paper or aluminum foil. Draw two 9-inch circles on the paper.

2. Beat the egg whites and 1 teaspoon of the lemon juice in a clean bowl with an electric mixer until they hold soft peaks. Add ¾ cup of the sugar a spoonful at a time, beating continuously until all the sugar is incorporated and the meringue holds stiff peaks and is shiny.

3. Divide the meringue between the two circles and spread evenly to the edges. Bake for 4 hours, then turn off the oven. Leave the meringues in the oven until they're cold. The meringues may be made up to a day ahead of time, covered, and stored in a dry place.

4. Combine the margarine and cocoa in a saucepan and cook over low heat for 3 minutes, stirring constantly. Do not burn. Pour

the hot milk into the cocoa mixture, stirring constantly with a wire whisk. Add ½ cup of the sugar and the coffee granules and simmer, stirring constantly, until thick. Remove from the heat, add the vanilla, and mix well. Allow the sauce to cool, then refrigerate for at least 2 hours. When ready to use, beat the mixture until fluffy and lighter in color. Spread over one meringue disk and sandwich the two meringues together.

5. To make the raspberry sauce, puree the raspberries in a food processor or blender. Pour through a strainer into a bowl and stir in the remaining ¼ cup of sugar and 1 teaspoon of lemon juice. To serve, cut the meringue cake into wedges and spoon a scant 2 tablespoons of raspberry sauce over each wedge. Garnish as desired.

MAKES ONE 9-INCH CAKE; 10 SERVINGS

Each serving contains approximately: Calories: 180; Grams of fat: 4; Cholesterol: negligible; Sodium: 61 mg

German Chocolate Cake

2 cups all-purpose unbleached flour
1½ cups firmly packed dark brown sugar
2 teaspoons baking soda
2 teaspoons baking powder
2 cups water
⅔ cup unsweetened cocoa powder
½ cup (1 stick) corn oil margarine
¼ cup nonfat plain yogurt
Coconut Topping (recipe follows)

1. Preheat the oven to 375°F. Combine the flour, sugar, baking soda, and baking powder in a large bowl and mix well. In a saucepan, combine the water, cocoa powder, and margarine. Cook over medium-low heat, stirring constantly, until the margarine is melted and the cocoa dissolved. Add the cocoa mixture to the dry ingredients and mix just until moistened. Add the yogurt and fold it in gently just until blended.

2. Pour the mixture into a 9 x 13-inch pan sprayed with non-stick vegetable spray. Bake until a knife inserted in the center of the cake comes out clean, 40 to 45 minutes. Cool completely before topping.

3. Spread the topping on the cooled cake and broil 6 inches from the heat until lightly browned, 2 to 3 minutes. Watch carefully to avoid scorching.

MAKES 16 SERVINGS

Each serving (cake only) contains approximately: Calories: 167; Grams of fat: 6.3; Cholesterol: negligible; Sodium: 77 mg

Coconut Topping

This is not a "light" recipe since it contains coconut, which is a highly saturated fat. However, it is the classic frosting for German Chocolate Cake *and* you only get 1½ teaspoons of coconut per serving.

2 tablespoons corn oil margarine
½ cup firmly packed dark brown sugar
¼ cup chopped walnuts
½ cup unsweetened shredded coconut
3 tablespoons nonfat milk
½ teaspoon pure vanilla extract

Melt the margarine in a small saucepan. Add the sugar, bring to a boil, and boil gently over medium heat for 2 minutes. Add the walnuts, coconut, and milk and boil for 1 more minute, stirring constantly. Remove from the heat and stir in the vanilla.

MAKES ABOUT 1 CUP

Each 1-tablespoon serving contains approximately: Calories: 42; Grams of fat: 2.7; Cholesterol: negligible; Sodium: 3 mg

Guilt–Free Chocolate Cake with Seven–Minute Almond Icing

This is a truly sensational fat-free cake that is amazingly rich-looking and even more amazingly rich-tasting! I developed this cake for *Cooking Healthy* magazine and it immediately became a big hit with my family and friends.

1 tablespoon instant coffee granules
1 cup boiling water
1 cup unsweetened cocoa powder
2 cups all-purpose unbleached flour
2 cups sugar
2 teaspoons baking soda
1 teaspoon baking powder
¼ teaspoon salt
1 cup nonfat milk
Three 2½-ounce jars baby-food pureed prunes
1 tablespoon pure vanilla extract
½ teaspoon pure almond extract
4 large egg whites
1 recipe Seven-minute Almond Icing (recipe follows; optional)
Confectioners' sugar for dusting (optional)
¼ cup sliced almonds, toasted in a 350°F oven until golden brown, 8
*   to 10 minutes (optional)*

1. Preheat the oven to 350°F. Spray a 9 x 13-inch pan with nonstick vegetable spray and set aside. Combine the instant coffee and boiling water and stir until the coffee has completely dissolved. Set aside.

2. Sift the cocoa into a large bowl. Add the flour, sugar, baking soda, baking powder, and salt and mix well. In another bowl combine the dissolved coffee, milk, prunes, extracts, and egg whites and mix well. Add the liquid ingredients to the dry ingredients and mix well.

3. Pour the batter into the prepared pan and bake until a knife inserted into the center of the cake comes out clean, about 30 minutes.

4. Allow the cake to cool in the pan on a rack for 10 minutes, then invert it onto a serving plate and allow to cool completely. Frost with the icing, or dust with confectioners' sugar. If desired, sprinkle the toasted almonds over the top of the icing.

MAKES 24 SERVINGS

Each serving (with icing) contains approximately: Calories: 180; Grams of fat: 1.4; Cholesterol: negligible; Sodium: 159 mg

Chocolate Torte

When you're looking for a great make-ahead dessert for a dinner party, this easy-to-make chocolate torte is the perfect answer. It is good served alone or with a fresh fruit or vanilla sauce.

2 envelopes unflavored gelatin
½ cup cool water
1½ cups boiling water
¾ cup unsweetened cocoa powder
¼ cup (½ stick) corn oil margarine, at room temperature
6 large egg whites
½ cup sugar
One 8-ounce angel food cake, cut into small pieces

1. In a large bowl, combine the gelatin and cool water and allow to stand 5 minutes. Add the boiling water and stir until the gelatin has completely dissolved. Add the cocoa powder and margarine and stir until the margarine has completely melted. Set aside to cool.

2. Beat the egg whites with an electric mixer until foamy. Add the sugar a little at a time and beat until soft peaks form. Fold the egg whites into the cooled cocoa mixture. Fold in the angel food cake and pour into a 10-inch springform pan sprayed with nonstick

vegetable spray. Refrigerate for several hours or overnight. To serve, unmold and slice into 8 pieces.

MAKES ONE 10-INCH CAKE; 8 SERVINGS

Each serving contains approximately: Calories: 210; Grams of fat: 7; Cholesterol: 0; Sodium: 120 mg

Seven-Minute Almond Icing

3 large egg whites
¼ cup water
1½ cups firmly packed light brown sugar
1 teaspoon cream of tartar
2 teaspoons pure vanilla extract
1 teaspoon pure almond extract

In the top of a double boiler combine the egg whites, water, sugar, and cream of tartar and mix well. Place over simmering water and, using an electric mixer, beat until stiff peaks form, about 5 minutes. Add the extracts and beat 2 more minutes. Remove from the heat and allow to cool slightly before icing the cake.

MAKES 4 CUPS

Low-Fat Cheesecake

6 zwieback crackers, crushed into fine crumbs
1 cup light sour cream, at room temperature
Two 8-ounce packages low-fat cream cheese, at room temperature
½ cup sugar
2 tablespoons all-purpose unbleached flour
2 teaspoons fresh lemon juice
2 teaspoons pure vanilla extract
¼ cup nonfat liquid egg substitute
3 large egg whites

1. Preheat the oven to 325°F. Sprinkle ¼ cup of the zwieback crumbs in the bottom of an 8-inch springform pan, reserving the remaining crumbs to sprinkle over the top of the cake.

2. Combine the sour cream, cream cheese, and ¼ cup of the sugar in a large bowl and mix until smooth and creamy. Stir in the flour a little at a time. Add the lemon juice and vanilla and mix well. Slowly stir in the egg substitute.

3. In a medium-size bowl, beat the egg whites with an electric mixer until they hold soft peaks. Then beat in the remaining ¼ cup of sugar until dissolved. Add one third of the beaten egg whites to the cheese mixture and mix well. Carefully fold the remaining egg whites into the mixture using a rubber spatula.

4. Spoon the mixture into the pan, being careful not to move the crumbs on the bottom. Sprinkle the remaining zwieback crumbs evenly over the top. Place the cheesecake in the center of the oven and immediately turn the temperature down to 300°F. Bake for 1 hour. Turn the oven off, but do not open the door. Leave the cake in the oven for 1 more hour.

5. Remove the cake from the oven and cool on a rack for 15 minutes. Then run a knife along the inside of the pan. Release and remove the sides, leaving the cake sitting on the bottom of the pan. Allow the cake to cool to room temperature and then refrigerate until cold before serving.

MAKES ONE 8-INCH CAKE; 8 SERVINGS

Each serving contains approximately: Calories: 282; Grams of fat: 17.7; Cholesterol: 55 mg; Sodium: 285 mg

Virtuous Cheesecake

This practically fat-free cheesecake recipe was given to me by my friend Nancy Ann Chandler from Dallas. She told me that it is so deliciously rich and creamy that none of my guests would ever believe how "virtuous" it truly is. The first time I made it I could hardly believe it myself. Fortunately she also told me not to worry if there were cracks on the top. There were—so I just followed her advice and covered them up with sliced strawberries! For an easy and unusual holiday dessert, use one 16-ounce can of whole-berry cranberry sauce in place of the strawberries on the top.

½ cup graham cracker crumbs
Two 8-ounce packages nonfat cream cheese
½ cup sugar
1 tablespoon all-purpose unbleached flour
½ cup nonfat sour cream
3 large egg whites
1 teaspoon pure vanilla extract
2 cups sliced fresh strawberries (optional)

1. Preheat the oven to 325°F. Spray a 9-inch pie plate with nonstick vegetable spray. Add the graham cracker crumbs and shake the plate to coat the entire surface. Set aside.

2. Combine the cream cheese, sugar, and flour in a large bowl. Beat with an electric mixer on medium speed until thoroughly mixed and creamy. Beat in sour cream, egg whites, and vanilla. Pour the mixture into the graham cracker-lined pie plate and place in the center of the oven. Bake for 40 minutes.

3. Remove from the oven and cool on a rack. Refrigerate for 3 hours before serving. There will be cracks in the top. If you wish to cover them before serving, just spoon the strawberries over the top.

MAKES ONE 9-INCH CAKE; 8 SERVINGS

Each serving contains approximately: Calories: 142;
Grams of fat: negligible; Cholesterol: 10 mg; Sodium: 391 mg

Blueberry Cheesecake

This recipe is very similar to that for Virtuous Cheesecake. However, there are just enough changes that doing it only as a variation became a bit confusing so I decided to include it as a separate recipe.

½ cup graham cracker crumbs
Two 8-ounce packages nonfat cream cheese
½ cup sugar
1 tablespoon all-purpose unbleached flour
½ cup nonfat sour cream
3 large egg whites
1 teaspoon pure vanilla extract
One 16-ounce package frozen unsweetened blueberries
Fresh mint sprigs (optional)

1. Preheat the oven to 325°F. Spray a 10-inch pie plate with nonstick vegetable spray. Add the graham cracker crumbs and shake the plate to coat the entire surface. Set aside.

2. Combine the cream cheese, sugar, and flour in a large bowl. Beat with an electric mixer on medium speed until thoroughly mixed and creamy. Beat in the sour cream, egg whites, and vanilla. Add half (1½ cups) of the unthawed blueberries and carefully fold them into the cheese mixture. Pour the mixture into the graham cracker-lined pie plate and place in the center of the oven. Bake for 45 minutes.

3. Remove from the oven and cool on a rack. Refrigerate for 3 hours before serving. Place the remaining 1½ cups of frozen blueberries in the refrigerator to thaw. To serve, top the cheesecake with the thawed blueberries and cut into 8 pie-shaped wedges. Garnish each serving with a mint sprig if desired.

MAKES ONE 9-INCH CAKE; 8 SERVINGS

Each serving contains approximately: Calories: 171; Grams of fat: negligible; Cholesterol: 10 mg; Sodium: 392 mg

Pumpkin Cheesecake

2 teaspoons corn oil margarine
8 graham cracker squares, crushed
2½ pounds low-fat ricotta cheese
1 cup sugar
1 large egg white
1 teaspoon canola oil
1 teaspoon nonfat dry milk
3 tablespoons all-purpose unbleached flour
2 teaspoons ground cinnamon
¼ teaspoon ground cloves
1 teaspoon ground ginger
¾ cup canned evaporated skim milk
1 tablespoon pure vanilla extract
One 16-ounce can solid pack pumpkin

1. Preheat the oven to 400°F. Spread the margarine evenly over the bottom and sides of a 9-inch springform pan. Add the graham cracker crumbs and rotate the pan to evenly coat the entire inside of the pan with the crumbs (more crumbs will end up on the bottom of pan). Set aside.

2. Combine the remaining ingredients in a food processor and blend until satin smooth. Pour the mixture into the prepared crust and bake for 15 minutes. Reduce the oven temperature to 275°F and bake an additional 1¼ hours. Turn off the heat but leave the cake in the oven for several hours to cool. Remove from the oven, cover, and refrigerate before serving.

MAKES ONE 9-INCH CAKE; 20 SERVINGS

Each serving contains approximately: Calories: 157; Grams of fat: 5;
Cholesterol: 18 mg; Sodium: 110 mg

Breakfast Bread Pudding Muffins

This is a recipe I developed for the California Raisin Board about a year ago and subsequently ran in my Cook It Light column. I received more fan mail from my readers telling me how fabulous they thought these muffins were than I have ever received for any other recipe. They are great for breakfast and also make a wonderful portable dessert for picnics and sack lunches. They are so easy to make that even very young children can learn to make them safely. They also freeze extremely well.

1½ cups nonfat milk
4 large egg whites
¼ cup sugar
1 tablespoon ground cinnamon
1 tablespoon pure vanilla extract
2 tablespoons corn oil margarine, melted
⅔ cup dark raisins
12 slices whole-wheat bread, cut into ½-inch cubes

1. Preheat the oven to 350°F. In a large bowl, combine all the ingredients except the raisins and cubed bread and mix well. Add the raisins and bread, mix well, and allow to soak for 5 minutes.

2. Spray a standard-size muffin tin or 12 custard cups with nonstick vegetable spray. Mound the mixture into each of the 12 cups. Bake until firm and well browned, about 35 minutes. Cool on a wire rack for at least 10 minutes before removing the muffins from the cups.

MAKES 12 MUFFINS

Each muffin contains approximately: Calories: 150; Grams of fat: 2.7; Cholesterol: 1 mg; Sodium: 183 mg

Cookies

Cookies are the most difficult category of sweets and desserts to revise because it is the fat content that gives them their crispness. Therefore, if you reduce the fat too much, you lose the texture or "mouth feel" of the original recipe. However, I think you will find all of the various types of cookies, bars, and squares in this section to be very satisfying and recipes that you will use over and over again.

I find that lining a baking sheet with parchment paper works better for most cookies than spraying it with a nonstick vegetable spray. On a sprayed sheet the bottoms of the cookies tend to get too brown before the tops are brown enough. Also, using the paper makes cleaning up a lot easier!

Chocolate Rum Drop Cookies

¾ cup (1½ sticks) corn oil margarine, softened
1½ cups all-purpose unbleached flour
½ cup unsweetened cocoa powder
¾ cup sugar
1 teaspoon baking powder
¼ teaspoon salt
1 tablespoon pure vanilla extract
½ teaspoon pure rum extract
¼ cup nonfat liquid egg substitute

1. Preheat the oven to 350°F. Put the softened margarine in a large bowl. Combine the flour, cocoa, sugar, baking powder, and salt and mix well. Add the flour mixture to the softened margarine and mix thoroughly, using a fork or a pastry blender.

2. Combine the extracts and egg substitute and mix well. Add to the flour mixture and mix thoroughly. The dough will be stiff and difficult to mix. When it is thoroughly mixed, make cookies 1½ inches in diameter (the size of a silver dollar) and space them evenly on ungreased cookie sheets. Bake for 15 minutes or until the bottoms are just starting to brown. Cool and carefully remove with a spatula to a serving plate.

MAKES 48 COOKIES

Each cookie contains approximately: Calories: 156; Grams of fat: 3; Cholesterol: 0; Sodium: 0

Gingersnaps

These spicy cookies are good eaten just as they are and they make an interesting crust when used in place of graham crackers for cheesecakes.

⅓ cup (⅔ stick) corn oil margarine
½ cup sugar
¼ cup nonfat liquid egg substitute or 2 large egg whites
¼ cup dark molasses
2 cups whole-wheat pastry or all-purpose flour
2 teaspoons baking soda
¼ teaspoon salt
1 teaspoon ground cinnamon
1 teaspoon ground cloves
½ teaspoon ground ginger
1 tablespoon sugar for sprinkling (optional)

1. Preheat the oven to 300°F. In a large bowl, cream the margarine and sugar together. Add the egg substitute and molasses and mix well.

2. In another bowl, combine the flour, baking soda, salt, and spices. Add the dry ingredients to the liquid ingredients and mix well.

3. Drop the cookie dough by small rounded teaspoonsful on an ungreased cookie sheet. If desired, sprinkle each cookie lightly with sugar. Bake until golden brown, about 15 minutes.

MAKES 3 DOZEN COOKIES

Each serving of four cookies contains approximately: Calories: 227; Grams of fat: 7; Cholesterol: 0; Sodium: 259 mg

Oatmeal Cookies

1 cup (2 sticks) corn oil margarine
¾ cup firmly packed dark brown sugar
½ cup granulated sugar
2 large egg whites
1 teaspoon pure vanilla extract
1½ cups whole-wheat flour
1 teaspoon ground cinnamon
1 teaspoon baking soda
1 teaspoon baking powder
¼ teaspoon freshly grated nutmeg
½ teaspoon salt
1½ cups quick-cooking or old-fashioned rolled oats
½ cup oat bran

1. Preheat the oven to 375°F. Cream together the margarine and sugars in a large bowl until light and fluffy. Beat in the egg whites and vanilla.

2. Combine the flour, cinnamon, baking soda, baking powder, nutmeg, and salt. Add to the margarine mixture, mixing well. Stir in the oats and oat bran.

3. Drop by rounded tablespoonsful onto an ungreased cookie sheet. Bake until lightly browned, about 10 minutes. Remove to a wire cooling rack.

MAKES 4 DOZEN 3-INCH COOKIES

Oatmeal Raisin Cookies:

Add ⅔ cup dark raisins when you add the oats and oat bran.

Each cookie contains approximately: Calories: 95; Grams of fat: 5; Cholesterol: 0; Sodium: 109 mg

Applesauce Oatmeal Cookies

The recipe for these delicious cookies was developed by Mott's applesauce for their Bake Lite program. It is a wonderful example of how you can use applesauce to replace most of the fat called for in baked goods without sacrificing quality in either taste or texture.

1 cup all-purpose unbleached flour
1 teaspoon baking powder
½ teaspoon baking soda
½ teaspoon salt
2 tablespoons vegetable shortening
¼ cup unsweetened cinnamon applesauce
½ cup granulated sugar
½ cup firmly packed light brown sugar
1 large egg or ¼ cup nonfat liquid egg substitute
1 teaspoon pure vanilla extract
1½ cups old-fashioned rolled oats (not quick-cooking)
½ cup dark raisins

1. Preheat the oven to 375°F. Lightly spray a cookie sheet with nonstick vegetable spray.

2. In a small bowl, mix the flour, baking powder, baking soda, and salt together.

3. In a large bowl, whisk together the shortening, applesauce, sugars, egg, and vanilla until the shortening breaks into pea-sized pieces.

4. Add the flour mixture to the applesauce mixture. Mix well. Fold in the oats, then the raisins.

5. Drop by rounded teaspoonsful onto the cookie sheet 2 inches apart. Bake for 10 to 12 minutes. Remove from the oven and cool on the cookie sheet for 5 minutes. Remove from the sheet and place on a cooling rack.

MAKES 36 COOKIES

Each cookie contains approximately: Calories: 53; Grams of fat: 1; Cholesterol: 6; Sodium: 46

Raisin Spice Cookies

1 cup dark raisins
⅔ cup sugar
¼ cup (½ stick) corn oil margarine
¼ cup buttermilk
½ cup nonfat liquid egg substitute
1 teaspoon pure vanilla extract
2 cups all-purpose unbleached flour
1 teaspoon baking powder
1 teaspoon baking soda
½ teaspoon salt
1 teaspoon ground cinnamon
1 teaspoon ground cloves

1. Preheat the oven to 375°F. Boil the raisins in water to cover for 2 minutes, then drain, reserving ⅔ cup of the liquid.

2. Combine the sugar, margarine, and buttermilk in a large bowl and blend until smooth and creamy. Add the egg substitute and vanilla and mix well. In a separate bowl, combine the dry ingredients. Add the dry ingredients, reserved raisin liquid, and raisins to the creamed mixture and mix well.

3. Drop the dough by teaspoonsful on an ungreased cookie sheet and bake until lightly browned, 8 to 10 minutes.

MAKES 3 DOZEN 2½-INCH COOKIES

Each cookie contains approximately: Calories: 66; Grams of fat: 2; Cholesterol: negligible; Sodium: 100 mg

Peanut Butter Cookies

When you are buying unhomogenized peanut butter in the market you should know that it is also called "old-fashioned" peanut butter on some labels. You can also make it yourself just by grinding up roasted peanuts in a food processor to the desired consistency.

¼ cup (½ stick) corn oil margarine
¾ cup granulated sugar
¾ cup firmly packed dark brown sugar
1 teaspoon pure vanilla extract
1 large egg plus 2 large egg whites, slightly beaten
3 cups all-purpose unbleached flour
2 teaspoons baking soda
Dash salt
1 cup unhomogenized (old-fashioned) peanut butter

1. Preheat the oven to 375°F. In a food processor or with an electric mixer, combine the margarine and sugars. Add the vanilla, egg, and egg whites and mix well.

2. Combine the flour, baking soda, and salt and add to the margarine mixture. Add the peanut butter and mix well.

3. Drop by tablespoonsful onto an ungreased cookie sheet and flatten with a fork. Bake until lightly browned, about 10 minutes.

MAKES 5½ DOZEN COOKIES

Each serving of 2 cookies contains approximately: Calories: 138;
Grams of fat: 6; Cholesterol: 8 mg; Sodium: 82 mg

Banana Drop Cookies

¾ cup plus 2 tablespoons sugar
½ cup (1 stick) corn oil margarine
1½ teaspoons pure vanilla extract
½ cup nonfat liquid egg substitute
3 ripe bananas, peeled and mashed (about 1 cup)
2½ cups cake flour
2 teaspoons baking powder
¼ teaspoon baking soda
¼ teaspoon salt
⅓ cup walnuts, chopped and toasted in a 350°F oven until golden
    brown, 8 to 10 minutes
¼ teaspoon ground cinnamon

1. Preheat the oven to 400°F. Line a baking sheet with parchment paper or spray it with nonstick vegetable spray. Beat ¾ cup of the sugar, margarine, and vanilla together in a large bowl until light and fluffy. Add the egg substitute and beat well. Stir in the bananas.

2. Sift the flour, baking powder, baking soda, and salt together, then add to the liquid ingredients and mix well. Stir in the walnuts. Drop by rounded teaspoonful 2 inches apart on the prepared baking sheet.

3. Combine the remaining 2 tablespoons sugar with the cinnamon and sprinkle each cookie with the mixture. Bake until puffed and lightly browned, 8 to 10 minutes.

MAKES 5 DOZEN COOKIES

Each cookie contains approximately: Calories: 57; Grams of fat: 2.5;
Cholesterol: 0; Sodium: 29mg

Cranberry Bars

During the holidays these delicious bars make wonderful host or hostess gifts.

1½ cups plus 2 tablespoons all-purpose unbleached flour
1 tablespoon granulated sugar
One 16-ounce can whole-berry cranberry sauce
1 tablespoon fresh lemon juice
1 teaspoon grated orange rind
1½ cups old-fashioned rolled oats (not quick-cooking)
½ cup firmly packed light brown sugar
¼ cup chopped walnuts, toasted in a 350°F oven until golden brown,
* 8 to 10 minutes*
½ teaspoon baking soda
1 teaspoon ground cinnamon
⅛ teaspoon salt
⅔ cup unsalted corn oil margarine, softened
⅓ cup buttermilk
1 large egg white, lightly beaten

1. In a small bowl, stir together 2 tablespoons of the flour and the granulated sugar. Set aside.

2. In a heavy, medium-size saucepan over medium-high heat, bring the cranberry sauce to a boil, stirring often. Stir in the flour and sugar mixture, reduce the heat to low, and simmer the cranberry mixture, stirring frequently, until the mixture is slightly thickened, about 5 minutes. Remove the pan from the heat and stir in the lemon juice and orange rind. Set aside to cool slightly.

3. Preheat the oven to 350°F. In a large bowl, stir together the oats, the remaining 1½ cups flour, brown sugar, toasted walnuts, baking soda, cinnamon, and salt. Using a wooden spoon, stir in the margarine, buttermilk, and egg white until the mixture is well combined and crumbly. Using your fingers, press half of the dough firmly and evenly onto the bottom of a 9 x 13-inch baking pan sprayed with nonstick vegetable spray. Spread the cranberry filling

evenly over the dough. Sprinkle the remaining dough evenly over the cranberry filling.

4. Bake until the top layer is light brown, 30 to 35 minutes. Place the pan on a wire rack to cool completely. With a sharp knife, cut into 24 bars. Store in an airtight container.

MAKES 24 BARS

Each bar contains approximately: Calories: 166; Grams of fat: 7; Cholesterol: negligible; Sodium: 43 mg

Peachy Almond Bars

This recipe is a revision I did for a reader in Canada. She said that while she liked peaches best in these bars, apricots could be substituted if peaches were not available.

½ cup almonds, chopped
2 cups (12 ounces) dried peaches, coarsely chopped
1 cup whole-wheat flour
1 large egg
2 large egg whites
3 tablespoons firmly packed dark brown sugar
¼ teaspoon salt
1 tablespoon pure vanilla extract
1 teaspoon pure almond extract
3 tablespoons canola oil
One 20-ounce can crushed pineapple packed in natural juice, drained

1. Preheat the oven to 350°F. Spray a standard 9 x 5-inch loaf pan with nonstick vegetable spray and set aside.

2. Place the chopped almonds on a baking sheet and bake until golden brown, 8 to 10 minutes. Watch carefully, they burn easily.

3. Combine the toasted almonds, peaches, and flour in a large bowl and mix well. Set aside.

4. In another bowl, beat the egg and egg whites together with a fork until frothy. Add the sugar, salt, extracts, and oil and mix well. Add the drained pineapple and again mix well.

5. Pour the liquid into the dry ingredients and mix well. Pour the batter into the prepared loaf pan and bake until a knife inserted in the center comes out clean, about 1 hour. Remove from the oven and place on a rack to cool to room temperature. To slice, turn out of the pan and cut in half lengthwise, then cut each half into sixteen ½-inch bars.

MAKES 32 BARS

Each bar contains approximately: Calories: 83; Grams of fat: 2.8; Cholesterol: 7; Sodium: 25

Fruit and Nut Bars

This recipe was developed by the Washington Apple Commission and it is a great dessert for picnics and sack lunches.

1 cup all-purpose unbleached flour
1 cup quick-cooking rolled oats
⅔ cup firmly packed dark brown sugar
2 teaspoons baking soda
½ teaspoon salt
½ teaspoon ground cinnamon
⅔ cup buttermilk
3 tablespoons vegetable oil
2 large egg whites, lightly beaten
1 Golden Delicious apple, cored (not peeled) and chopped
½ cup dried cranberries or dark raisins, chopped
¼ cup chopped nuts

1. Preheat the oven to 375°F. Combine the flour, oats, sugar, baking soda, salt, and cinnamon in a large bowl and mix well.

2. Add the buttermilk, oil, and egg whites and beat with an electric mixer just until well blended. Stir in the apple, dried fruit, and nuts and spread evenly in a 9-inch-square baking pan that has been sprayed with nonstick vegetable spray. Place in the center of the oven and bake until a knife inserted in the center comes out clean, 20 to 25 minutes. Cool and cut into 10 bars.

MAKES 10 BARS

Each bar contains approximately: Calories: 232; Grams of fat: 7; Cholesterol: negligible; Sodium: 298 mg

Date Bars

These bars are a truly moist and delicious version of this old-fashioned favorite. They can be made ahead and frozen in individual plastic bags, which are perfect for sack lunches.

½ cup nonfat liquid egg substitute
¾ cup sugar
¼ cup (½ stick) corn oil margarine, melted
1 teaspoon pure vanilla extract
One 8-ounce box chopped dates (1½ cups)
¼ cup chopped walnuts, toasted in a 350°F oven until golden brown, 8 to 10 minutes
½ cup plus 2 tablespoons all-purpose unbleached flour
¼ teaspoon baking powder
¼ teaspoon salt
2 tablespoons confectioners' sugar

1. Preheat the oven to 325°F. Spray a 9 x 13-inch baking pan with nonstick vegetable spray.

2. Pour the egg substitute into a large bowl and gradually beat in the sugar. Add the melted margarine and vanilla and mix well. Stir in the dates and walnuts.

3. In a separate bowl, combine the flour, baking powder, and salt. Add this to the liquid mixture and mix well. Pour the batter into the prepared pan. Bake until the top is lightly browned, 30 to 35 minutes.

4. Cool completely before cutting. Cut into 48 bars and roll in the confectioners' sugar.

MAKES 48 BARS

Each bar contains approximately: Calories: 51; Grams of fat: 1.7; Cholesterol: 0; Sodium: 18 mg

Carrot Bars

1 cup all-purpose unbleached flour
1 teaspoon baking powder
¾ teaspoon ground cinnamon
½ cup firmly packed dark brown sugar
¼ cup honey
3 tablespoons canola oil
1 large egg
1 large egg white
1 teaspoon pure vanilla extract
2 large carrots, grated (1½ cups)
¼ cup pecan halves, toasted in a 350°F oven until golden brown, 8
    to 10 minutes

FOR THE GLAZE
⅔ cup confectioners' sugar
4½ teaspoons water
½ teaspoon pure vanilla extract

1. Preheat the oven to 350°F. Spray a 9 x 13-inch baking pan with nonstick vegetable spray. Combine the flour, baking powder, and cinnamon in a small bowl. Mix well and set aside.

2. In a large bowl combine the sugar, honey, oil, egg, egg white, and vanilla. Using an electric mixer, beat until well mixed. At low speed beat in the flour mixture a little at a time. Stir in the carrots and pecans. Pour the batter into the prepared pan and bake until the center springs back when lightly touched, about 25 minutes.

3. While the cake is baking, combine the glaze ingredients in a small bowl and mix well. While the cake is still warm, spread the glaze quickly and evenly over the top. Cool completely on a rack before cutting into 48 bars.

MAKES 48 BARS

Each bar contains approximately: Calories: 39; Grams of fat: 1.4; Cholesterol: 4 mg; Sodium: 12 mg

Apple Cheddar Scones

These tasty scones were developed by the Washington Apple Commission and they suggest using small Rome apples. If you can't find them in your market, then just use Golden Delicious. Unlike traditional scone recipes which call for generous amounts of butter and cream, this version is leaner and lighter, but has a wonderful rich flavor.

1½ cups all-purpose unbleached flour
½ cup toasted wheat germ
3 tablespoons sugar
2 teaspoons baking powder
½ teaspoon salt
2 tablespoons butter
1 small Rome apple, cored and chopped
¼ cup grated sharp cheddar cheese
1 large egg white
½ cup low-fat milk

1. Preheat the oven to 400°F. Combine the flour, wheat germ, sugar, baking powder, and salt in a medium-size bowl. Using a pastry blender or two knives, cut the butter in until the mixture has the consistency of coarse crumbs. Toss the chopped apple and cheese with the mixture.

2. Beat together the egg white and milk until well combined. Add to the flour mixture, mixing with a fork until a dough forms. Turn the dough out onto a lightly floured surface and knead six times.

3. Spread the dough evenly in an 8-inch round cake pan sprayed with nonstick vegetable spray and score deeply with a knife into 6 wedges. Place in the center of the oven and bake until the top springs back when gently pressed, 25 to 30 minutes. Allow to stand for at least 5 minutes before removing from the pan.

MAKES 6 SCONES

Each scone contains approximately: Calories: 255; Grams of fat: 7; Cholesterol: 16 mg; Sodium: 357 mg

Almond Macaroons

Unlike most macaroons, these tasty little treats contain no coconut and are therefore very low in both calories and fat.

¾ cup almonds
¾ cup quick-cooking rolled oats
⅓ cup sugar
2 large egg whites
1 teaspoon pure vanilla extract
1 teaspoon pure coconut extract
½ teaspoon pure almond extract

1. Preheat the oven to 350°F. Line a baking sheet with parchment paper. (Using a baking sheet sprayed with nonstick vegetable

spray does not work as well as the paper because the bottoms of the cookies tend to get too brown before the tops are lightly browned.)

2. Combine the almonds and oats in a food processor and reduce to a meallike consistency.

3. In a large bowl whisk together the sugar and egg whites until foamy. Add all of the extracts and mix well. Add the dry mixture and mix well. Spoon the mixture, 1 teaspoon per cookie, onto the lined baking sheet and bake until lightly browned, about 15 minutes. Cool slightly, then transfer the cookies to a rack and cool completely.

MAKES 40 MACAROONS

Each macaroon contains approximately: Calories: 30; Grams of fat: 1.5; Cholesterol: 0; Sodium: 3 mg

Walnut Biscotti

Biscotti are more frequently made with almonds and therefore the walnuts offer a delightfully different flavor to these crunchy Italian cookies.

2 tablespoons finely chopped walnuts
1 tablespoon corn oil margarine
¼ cup sugar
2 large egg whites, lightly beaten
1 teaspoon pure almond extract
1 cup all-purpose unbleached flour
½ teaspoon baking powder
⅛ teaspoon salt

1. Preheat the oven to 375°F. Place the chopped walnuts on a baking pan and toast until they are a rich golden brown, 7 to 8 minutes. Watch them carefully as they burn easily. Set aside.

2. Combine the margarine and sugar, mixing until completely blended. Add the egg whites and extract and mix well.

3. In a large bowl, combine the flour, baking powder, and salt and mix well. Add the egg white mixture and toasted walnuts to the flour mixture and mix well.

4. Spoon the dough into a standard-size loaf pan that has been sprayed with nonstick vegetable spray. Spread evenly over the bottom of the pan by wetting your hands and pressing down on the dough. Place in the oven and bake until a knife inserted in the center comes out clean, about 15 minutes.

5. Remove from the oven and turn onto a cutting board. Just as soon as the loaf is cool enough to handle, cut it into sixteen ½-inch slices. Place the slices on a baking sheet either covered with parchment paper or sprayed with nonstick vegetable spray. Bake for 5 minutes, then turn the slices over and bake until golden brown on both sides, about 5 more minutes.

MAKES 16 SERVINGS

Each serving contains approximately: Calories: 55; Grams of fat: 1.4; Cholesterol: 0; Sodium: 37 mg

Cinnamon Sticks

These amusing looking and very low-fat sweet breadsticks are a real conversation piece as well as being truly delicious. They are wonderful served with coffee or tea as well as for dessert cookies.

⅔ cup low-fat milk, warmed
2 teaspoons baking powder
¼ cup sugar
½ teaspoon salt
1 tablespoon ground cinnamon
¾ cup whole-wheat flour
¾ cup all-purpose unbleached flour

1. Combine the warm milk, baking powder, sugar, salt, and cinnamon in a large bowl and mix well. Stir in the flours, then turn

onto a floured surface. Knead the dough until it becomes smooth and elastic, adding a little more flour if necessary, about 5 minutes. Cover the dough and allow it to rest at room temperature for 30 minutes.

2. Preheat the oven to 375°F. Divide the dough into 12 equal balls. Roll each ball into a long, thin rope. Place them on a baking sheet sprayed with nonstick vegetable spray, then lightly spray the tops of the sticks. Bake until the bottoms are golden brown, about 12 minutes. Turn the sticks over and bake until the other side is browned, about 10 minutes.

MAKES 12 STICKS

Each stick contains approximately: Calories: 78;
Grams of fat: negligible; Cholesterol: 1 mg; Sodium: 165 mg

Fudge Brownies

In these delicious, rich-tasting brownies, pureed prunes replace the butter or oil called for in other recipes, making them lower in both calories and fat than most brownies.

One 2½-ounce jar baby-food pureed prunes
¾ cup sugar
½ cup nonfat liquid egg substitute
¼ cup buttermilk
1 teaspoon pure vanilla extract
¾ cup all-purpose unbleached flour
⅓ cup unsweetened cocoa powder
¼ cup semisweet chocolate chips

1. Preheat the oven to 350°F. Spray an 8-inch square baking pan with nonstick vegetable spray and set aside. Combine the prunes and sugar in a bowl and mix well. Stir in the egg substitute, buttermilk, and vanilla. In another bowl combine the flour and cocoa powder and mix well, then add to the liquid ingredients. Stir in the chocolate chips and spoon the mixture into the prepared pan.

2. Bake in the preheated oven until the top springs back when touched, about 30 minutes. Be careful not to overbake. Cool on a rack for at least 30 minutes before cutting into 16 squares.

MAKES 16 BROWNIES

Each brownie contains approximately: Calories: 89; Grams of fat: 1.8; Cholesterol: 0; Sodium: 19 mg

Mocha Brownies

These are wonderfully rich and delicious brownies just as the recipe is written. However, if you like nuts in your brownies, I would suggest adding ⅓ cup of toasted chopped almonds, walnuts, or peanuts.

⅓ *cup corn oil margarine*
¾ *cup sugar*
½ *cup nonfat liquid egg substitute*
¼ *cup buttermilk*
1½ *teaspoons pure vanilla extract*
¾ *cup all-purpose unbleached flour*
⅓ *cup unsweetened cocoa powder*
2 *tablespoons instant coffee granules*
¼ *cup semisweet chocolate chips*
1 *teaspoon confectioners' sugar*

1. Preheat the oven to 350°F. Spray an 8-inch square baking pan with nonstick vegetable spray.

2. In a small saucepan, melt the margarine. Remove from the heat and stir in the sugar. Add the egg substitute, buttermilk, and vanilla and mix well.

3. In a medium-size bowl, combine the flour, cocoa, and instant coffee. Add to the liquid ingredients and mix well. Stir in the chocolate chips. Pour the batter into the prepared pan.

4. Bake until firm to the touch, about 30 minutes, being careful not to overbake. Cool and sift the confectioners' sugar over the top. Cut into squares.

MAKES 16 SQUARES

Each square contains approximately: Calories: 129; Grams of fat: 5.9; Cholesterol: 0; Sodium: 32 mg

Pumpkin Whoopee Pies

Whoopee pies are not really pies at all but filled cookies which are generally just loaded with fat and calories. This recipe is a revision of a really fat-loaded version and even though I have managed to reduce the calories from fat by over half, they are still not truly light. However, they are delicious and if you can limit the number of them you eat they can still be part of a prudent menu.

1¾ cups firmly packed dark brown sugar
½ cup canola oil
One 16-ounce can solid pack pumpkin
½ cup nonfat liquid egg substitute
1 teaspoon ground cinnamon
1 teaspoon ground ginger
½ teaspoon ground cloves
1 tablespoon pure vanilla extract
3 cups all-purpose unbleached flour
½ teaspoon salt
1 teaspoon baking powder
1 teaspoon baking soda
½ cup buttermilk
4 ounces low-fat cream cheese, softened
1 tablespoon corn oil margarine
2 cups confectioners' sugar, sifted

1. Preheat the oven to 350°F. Combine the brown sugar and oil in a large bowl and blend until smooth. Beat in the pumpkin, egg substitute, spices, and 1 teaspoon of the vanilla extract, mixing well.

2. In a separate bowl, combine the flour, salt, baking powder, and baking soda. Add it to the pumpkin mixture alternating with the buttermilk, mixing well.

3. Drop the batter by rounded tablespoonsful 2 inches apart on an ungreased baking sheet. With a spoon, spread the batter out into 2-inch flat circles. Bake until the tops of the cookies spring back when touched lightly, 10 to 12 minutes. Cool completely.

4. While the cookies are cooling, beat together the cream cheese, margarine, confectioners' sugar, and remaining 2 teaspoons of vanilla. Spread about 2 teaspoons of the cream-cheese mixture on the tops of each of half of the baked cookies and top with the remaining cookies. Store in the refrigerator.

MAKES ABOUT 28 "PIES"

Each "pie" contains approximately: Calories: 194; Grams of fat: 6; Cholesterol: 3 mg; Sodium: 135 mg

Sweet Bagel Balls

These tasty little balls make wonderful treats for both dessert and breakfast.

1 envelope active dry yeast (check the expiration date on envelope)
2 cups all-purpose unbleached flour
3 tablespoons nonfat dry milk
3 tablespoons sugar
1 teaspoon salt
2 teaspoons ground cinnamon
½ cup warm water
1 large egg
1 tablespoon canola oil
¼ cup dark raisins, rinsed in hot water
2 quarts boiling water
1 large egg white
1 tablespoon water

1. In a large bowl, combine the yeast, 1 cup of the flour, the dry milk, 2 tablespoons of the sugar, the salt, and cinnamon and mix well. Stir in the warm water, egg, and oil. Using an electric mixer, blend on low speed, then beat 3 minutes on high. Gradually add the rest of the flour, beating until a stiff dough forms. Knead until smooth and elastic, 8 to 10 minutes by hand or 6 minutes with a dough hook, adding more flour if needed. Knead in the raisins.

2. Place the dough in a bowl sprayed with nonstick vegetable spray and turn to coat the top. Cover the bowl with plastic wrap and a damp towel. Let the dough rise until doubled, about 45 minutes.

3. Turn the dough out onto a floured board. Divide into 24 equal balls and allow to rest for 10 minutes.

4. Preheat the oven to 425°F. Combine the boiling water and remaining sugar in a medium-size saucepan until simmering. Carefully place the bagel balls in the hot water and simmer gently over medium heat for 2 minutes on each side. Remove with a skimmer to a towel. Place on a baking sheet covered with parchment paper or sprayed with nonstick vegetable spray. Combine the egg white and water, beat lightly, and brush on the tops of the bagel balls. Bake about 15 minutes, turning the baking sheet halfway through to brown evenly. Remove to wire racks to cool.

MAKES 24 BAGEL BALLS

Each ball contains approximately: Calories: 62; Grams of fat: negligible; Cholesterol: 9 mg; Sodium: 109 mg

Chocolate Bagels

The only thing about making bagels that takes more time than ordinary bread is that you simmer them in water before baking. You can eliminate this step from any bagel recipe, but you'll end up with bialys. I happen to like bagels better than bialys because sealing them in the simmering water bath gives them a chewy texture not found in other breads.

When you make bagels, you can play with their sizes and

shapes. I like to make miniature chocolate bagels, cut them in half, and spread them with nonfat cream cheese for fat-free "cookies." These bagel "cookies" make wonderful treats for school and office sack lunches.

4 teaspoons decaffeinated instant coffee granules
½ cup boiling water
1 cup cool water
2 envelopes active dry yeast (check expiration date on envelopes)
⅔ cup plus 2 tablespoons sugar
3 cups all-purpose unbleached flour
¾ cup unsweetened cocoa powder
1 teaspoon salt
2 teaspoons ground cinnamon
4 teaspoons pure vanilla extract
2 quarts plus 1 tablespoon water
Cornmeal (optional)
1 large egg white

1. Dissolve the instant coffee in the boiling water. Add the cool water and mix well. Add the yeast and 1 tablespoon of the sugar; stir to mix well. Let stand until the yeast starts to bubble, 3 to 5 minutes.

2. While waiting for the yeast to bubble, combine 2 cups of the flour with the cocoa powder, salt, cinnamon, and ⅔ cup sugar and mix well. Pour in the yeast mixture and mix well. Add the vanilla and continue to mix. Slowly mix in as much of the remaining flour as is necessary for the dough to become firm enough to be shaped into a ball. (The dough will reach a point where it no longer accepts more flour being mixed into it.)

3. Move the dough to a floured board and knead it, adding as much flour as needed to make the dough smooth, firm, and elastic. Knead for 10 minutes. (If using a dough hook in a food processor, knead for 6 minutes or until the dough is the proper consistency.)

4. Place the dough ball in an oiled bowl and turn to oil the top. Cover with plastic wrap and a damp towel and allow to rise

until doubled in bulk, about 1 hour. Punch the dough down and turn onto a floured board. Divide the dough into 12 equal pieces. Shape each piece into a ball, then flatten each ball slightly with the palm of your hand. Press your thumbs into the center of each flattened ball and tear it open. Shape each one into a doughnut shape. Cover with plastic wrap and allow to rise slightly, 10 to 15 minutes.

5. Preheat the oven to 425°F. Heat the 2 quarts of water and the remaining 1 tablespoon of sugar in a saucepan just until the water is simmering. Carefully place the bagels, several at a time, in the water and simmer for 30 seconds, then turn over and simmer for another 30 seconds. Remove the bagels from the water and place them on paper towels to drain.

6. Lightly oil a baking sheet and sprinkle with cornmeal or line a baking sheet with parchment paper. Place the drained bagels on the baking sheet. Combine the egg white with the remaining 1 tablespoon of water and beat lightly. Brush the top of each bagel with the egg wash. Bake until browned, 20 to 25 minutes. Turn the baking sheet halfway through the baking time to ensure even browning.

MAKES 12 BAGELS

Variation:

To make miniature tea or "cookie" bagels, divide the dough into about 40 little bagels. Bake until browned, about 15 minutes.

Each bagel contains approximately: Calories: 185; Grams of fat: 1; Cholesterol: 0; Sodium: 203 mg

Cream Puffs

To me a cream puff is the ultimate cookie. They somehow always seem so festive and special. They are also both easy and fun to make and can be made ahead of time and frozen so that all you have to do is thaw them out and fill them and you have a truly impressive snack or dessert in minutes.

½ cup water
¼ cup (½ stick) corn oil margarine
½ cup all-purpose unbleached flour
2 teaspoons sugar
1 large egg
2 large egg whites
1 cup Custard Filling (recipe follows)

1. Preheat the oven to 375°F. Combine the water and margarine in a medium-size saucepan and bring to a boil. Combine the flour and sugar and add all at once to the boiling mixture. Over low heat, beat until the mixture leaves the sides of the pan and forms a ball. Remove from the heat and cool for 5 minutes. Add the egg and egg whites, one at a time, beating well after each addition. Continue beating until the mixture has a satinlike sheen.

2. Spray a large baking sheet with nonstick vegetable spray and arrange the batter in 8 equal mounds about 2 inches apart. Bake until lightly browned and puffed, about 40 minutes. Remove from the oven and immediately cut a slit in the side of each puff. Return to the oven for 5 more minutes. Remove from the oven and cool on a wire rack.

3. To serve, slit the cream puffs almost all of the way around or slice the tops off of each one and fill each with 2 tablespoons of the custard filling.

MAKES 8 SERVINGS

Each serving contains approximately: Calories: 139; Grams of fat: 7;
Cholesterol: 27 mg; Sodium: 117 mg

Custard Filling

This filling can also be used as a sauce on cakes, pies, or fruit.

1 cup nonfat milk
1 tablespoon cornstarch
3 tablespoons sugar
2 large egg whites, lightly beaten
1 teaspoon canola oil
¾ teaspoon pure vanilla extract

Combine the milk and cornstarch in a medium-size saucepan and mix until the cornstarch is completely dissolved. Add the sugar, egg whites, and oil and mix well. Slowly bring to a boil over medium-low heat, stirring constantly with a wire whisk until thickened. Remove from the heat and stir in the vanilla. Place plastic wrap over the top to keep a film from forming. Allow to cool to room temperature.

MAKES 1 CUP CUSTARD

Each 2-tablespoon serving contains approximately: Calories: 43; Grams of fat: negligible; Cholesterol: 1 mg; Sodium: 29 mg

Spa Baklava

This is a recipe that I developed for the Canyon Ranch Fitness Resorts several years ago and it is still a favorite of mine with Greek or Middle Eastern menus.

½ cup walnut halves
¼ cup (½ stick) corn oil margarine
½ cup honey
1 teaspoon ground cinnamon
Dash ground cloves

½ teaspoon pure vanilla extract
6 sheets phyllo dough, thawed according to package instructions

1. Preheat the oven to 250°F. Grind the walnuts to the consistency of fine gravel using a food processor fitted with the metal blade and set aside. Combine the margarine and ¼ cup of the honey in a small, heavy saucepan and cook over low heat until the margarine is completely melted. Add the cinnamon, cloves, and vanilla and mix thoroughly.

2. Spray a 10 x 14-inch baking sheet with nonstick vegetable spray. On a slightly damp towel, place one layer of the phyllo dough. Using a pastry brush, lightly brush the entire surface with the honey mixture. Add another layer of phyllo and repeat. Sprinkle the second layer with 1¼ tablespoons of the walnuts, leaving a bare edge along one end.

3. Using the towel to help roll the phyllo, roll up (as you would a jelly roll) toward the bare edge and close neatly. Place the roll on the baking sheet. Brush it with another light layer of the honey mixture and slice diagonally into 8 even portions, allowing for 2 half slices at the ends. Repeat the procedure two more times with the remaining sheets of phyllo dough. Bake until golden brown, about 40 minutes. Watch closely after 30 minutes because the rolls will brown suddenly. Cool on a rack.

4. When cool, warm the remaining ¼ cup honey and paint the honey on each roll with a pastry brush.

MAKES 3 ROLLS; 27 SERVINGS

Each serving contains approximately: Calories: 62; Grams of fat: 3.1;
Cholesterol: 0; Sodium: 30 mg

Crepes and Blintzes

You will find some very unusual dessert ideas in this section, such as Cornmeal Crepes and Puffed Cherry Pancakes. Many of the recipes, like Blueberry Blintzes and Honey Walnut Crepes, can also double very nicely for brunch entrees.

Crepes

This is a wonderfully easy basic crepe recipe. I use these crepes for several of the recipes in this chapter and for Vanilla Ice Milk Crepes with Caramel Sauce on page 224.

> 1 cup nonfat milk
> 1 large egg
> ½ cup whole-wheat flour
> ¼ cup all-purpose unbleached flour
> 1 tablespoon sugar
> ⅛ teaspoon salt

1. Combine all the ingredients in a blender and blend until well mixed.

2. Heat a nonstick crepe or omelet pan over medium heat until a drop of water dances on the surface. Spoon 2 tablespoons of the batter into the hot pan and roll it from side to side to cover the entire surface. When the edges curl away from the sides of the pan, turn the crepe over to lightly brown the other side. Repeat until all of the batter has been used. To keep crepes pliable, put them in a covered container as you make them. To freeze place a piece of plastic wrap, waxed paper, or aluminum foil between each crepe and wrap them airtight or place them in a large Ziploc bag.

MAKES 12 CREPES

Honey Crepes:

Substitute 1 tablespoon of honey for the sugar.

Cinnamon Crepes:

Add ½ teaspoon ground cinnamon in step 1.

Crepe Cups:

Preheat the oven to 350°F. Place each crepe in a custard cup or a muffin tin sprayed with nonstick vegetable spray and then lightly spray the crepe. Place them in the oven until crisp, about 5 minutes.

Each crepe contains approximately: Calories: 45; Grams of fat: 6.9; Cholesterol: 18 mg; Sodium: 41 mg

Cornmeal Crepes

I particularly like these "corny" crepes topped with fresh fruit for dessert, and one of my favorite brunch entrées is a sandwich made with these crepes, fresh strawberries, and low-fat ricotta cheese.

1 cup nonfat milk
2 large egg whites
½ cup yellow cornmeal
½ cup whole-wheat flour
3 tablespoons sugar
¾ teaspoon baking powder
½ teaspoon salt
1 tablespoon corn oil margarine

1. Combine all the ingredients except the margarine in a blender and process just until well mixed. Pour the batter into a bowl and allow to stand for 15 minutes.

2. Melt the margarine in a nonstick skillet or crepe pan over medium heat. Pour the melted margarine into the batter and mix well. Wipe the inner surface of the pan with a paper towel and place the pan back on the heat. For each crepe spoon 2 tablespoons of the batter into the pan and tilt it to spread the batter evenly over the entire inner surface of the pan. Cook until lightly browned, about 2 minutes per side. Follow the freezing directions on page 188.

MAKES 16 CREPES

Each crepe contains approximately: Calories: 52;
Grams of fat: negligible; Cholesterol: negligible; Sodium: 164 mg

Chocolate Crepes

For a really fast and delicious dessert, try filling these crepes with an all-fruit jam and topping it with a dollop of your favorite nonfat yogurt.

½ cup all-purpose unbleached flour
¼ cup unsweetened cocoa powder, sifted
2 tablespoons sugar
¼ teaspoon salt
1 cup nonfat milk
2 large egg whites, lightly beaten

1. Combine the flour and cocoa in a medium-size bowl. Add the sugar and salt and mix well. Add the milk, slowly beating with a whisk or an egg beater, then stir in the egg whites.

2. Heat a crepe pan over medium heat until a drop of water dances on the surface. Coat with nonstick vegetable spray and wipe the surface with a paper towel. Spoon 2 tablespoons of the batter into the pan and tilt the pan from side to side until the batter covers the surface of the pan. Cook until the edges curl, then flip over and cook the other side until lightly browned, about 3 minutes total. Keep cooked crepes in a covered container as you make the remaining ones to keep them pliable. If you are making them ahead of time or if you plan to freeze the crepes, place pieces of waxed paper or aluminum foil between them so they won't stick together. Seal tightly in freezer wrap, Baggies, or an airtight container. You can store them in the freezer for up to 6 months. You can serve these crepes as you would pancakes, roll them up for blintzes, or use them with my recipe for cinnamon-apple filling (recipe follows).

MAKES 12 CREPES

Each crepe contains approximately: Calories: 40; Grams of fat: 1; Cholesterol: negligible; Sodium: 69 mg

Chocolate Crepes with Cinnamon-Apple Filling and Vanilla Cream Spread

I have purposely divided this recipe into separate recipes and given nutritional information for each part. The cinnamon-apple filling is wonderful as a topping on puddings and ice cream and the vanilla cream spread is good on cakes and cookies—it's even good as a spread on breakfast toast!

FOR THE CINNAMON-APPLE FILLING
(MAKES 3 CUPS; TWELVE ¼-CUP SERVINGS)

2 tablespoons corn oil margarine
½ cup firmly packed dark brown sugar
¼ cup ground cinnamon
2 pounds Golden Delicious apples, peeled, cored, and thinly sliced
1 tablespoon pure vanilla extract
¼ cup fresh lemon juice

FOR THE VANILLA CREAM SPREAD
(MAKES ¾ CUP; TWELVE 1-TABLESPOON SERVINGS)

1 cup low-fat ricotta cheese
2 tablespoons sugar
1 teaspoon pure vanilla extract
1 recipe Chocolate Crepes (page 190)

1. To make the filling, melt the margarine in a large pan over medium heat. Add the brown sugar and cinnamon and mix well. Add the apples and cook, stirring occasionally, until they start to soften. Add the vanilla and lemon juice and cook until the apples are very soft. The total cooking time should not exceed 10 minutes. Set aside to cool.

2. To make the spread, combine all the ingredients in a food processor fitted with the metal blade and blend until satin smooth. Store, covered, in the refrigerator for up to several days.

3. To assemble the crepes, spoon ¼ cup of the filling down the center of each crepe. Fold the crepe over the filling, placing it seam

side down on a serving dish. Top each filled crepe with 1 table-spoon of the spread.

MAKES 12 SERVINGS

Each serving contains approximately: Calories: 181; filling, 103; spread, 38; Grams of fat: 4; filling, 2; spread, 2; Cholesterol: 7 mg; filling, 0; spread, 6; Sodium: 124 mg; filling, 29; spread, 26

Honey Walnut Crepes

This is a very rich-tasting, low-fat dessert. It is a perfect light dessert for after almost any kind of meal.

½ cup chopped walnuts
12 walnut halves
2 large egg whites
½ teaspoon cream of tartar
2 tablespoons water
3 tablespoons honey
½ cup firmly packed light brown sugar
1 teaspoon pure vanilla extract
½ teaspoon pure walnut extract
1 cup light sour cream
12 Honey Crepes (page 188)

1. Preheat the oven to 350°F. Spread the chopped walnuts and walnut halves on a baking sheet and toast until golden brown, about 8 minutes. Watch them carefully as they burn easily. Set aside.

2. In the top of a double boiler, combine the egg whites, cream of tartar, water, honey, and brown sugar. Mix well and place over simmering water. Using an electric mixer, beat the mixture until soft peaks form, about 4 minutes. Add the extracts and continue to beat for 2 more minutes. Remove from the heat and fold in the sour cream and then the toasted chopped walnuts, reserving the walnut halves to use as garnish.

3. Spoon 3 tablespoons of the honey mixture down the center of each crepe. Roll the crepe around the filling and place, seam side down, on a serving plate. Place about a 1-tablespoon dollop of the honey mixture on the top of each rolled crepe and place a toasted walnut half on top of the dollop for garnish.

MAKES 12 SERVINGS

Each serving contains approximately: Calories: 158; Grams of fat: 6;
Cholesterol: 26 mg; Sodium: 70 mg

Crepes "Suzette"

This is my "spa" version of this popular and classic French dessert. I originally designed it for the Canyon Ranch Fitness Resorts and I have served it many times since at my own dinner parties.

1 cup fresh orange juice
2 teaspoons arrowroot
2 tablespoons sugar
2 teaspoons grated orange rind
1 teaspoon corn oil margarine
¼ cup Grand Marnier or other orange-flavored liqueur
1 recipe Crepes (page 187)

1. Combine the orange juice and arrowroot in a saucepan and stir until the arrowroot is completely dissolved. Add the sugar and orange rind and mix well. Place over medium heat and bring to a boil. Reduce the heat to low and simmer, stirring constantly, until slightly thickened. Remove from the heat and stir in the margarine and Grand Marnier.

2. Arrange the crepes, folded in quarters, on a serving dish and spoon the sauce evenly over the top.

MAKES 12 SERVINGS

Each serving contains approximately: Calories: 72; Grams of fat: 1;
Cholesterol: 18 mg; Sodium: 41 mg

Soufflé-Filled Crepes

This is a variation on a recipe that I learned how to make at Le Cordon Bleu Cooking School in London. My version is a bit lighter, but still a truly delicious and impressive dessert.

FOR THE CREPES (MAKES 12 CREPES)

1¾ cups nonfat milk
2 tablespoons sugar
2¼ cups all-purpose unbleached flour
⅛ teaspoon salt
1 large egg plus 4 large egg whites, lightly beaten
2 tablespoon corn oil margarine, melted
2 tablespoons grated orange rind

FOR THE SOUFFLÉ

1 vanilla bean
1 cup low-fat milk
¼ cup plus 1 tablespoon sugar
1 large egg plus 6 large egg whites
2 tablespoons plus 2 teaspoons cornstarch
¼ cup Cointreau or other orange-flavored liqueur

FOR THE GARNISH

Confectioners' sugar for dusting
Fresh mint sprigs

1. To make the crepe batter, combine the milk and sugar in a small bowl and stir until the sugar is completely dissolved. Set aside.

2. In a large bowl, combine the flour and salt and mix well. Make a well in the center of the flour and pour in the lightly beaten egg and egg whites and mix well. Add the milk and sugar mixture and again mix well. Slowly stir in the melted margarine. Pour through a strainer, then stir in the grated orange rind. Allow to rest for 15 minutes before making the crepes.

3. To cook the crepes, heat a lightly oiled skillet or crepe pan over medium heat until water dances on the surface. Pour in ¼ cup

of the batter and tilt the pan to cover the surface. Cook until the edges start to curl. Turn over and cook just until lightly browned. Place the crepes in a covered dish as you make them to keep them pliable.

4. To make the soufflé, place the vanilla bean in the milk in a medium saucepan and heat to the boiling point. Combine ¼ cup of the sugar, the egg, and 2 of the egg whites in a bowl and mix until the sugar is completely dissolved. Add the cornstarch and mix well. Remove the vanilla bean from the hot milk and add half of the hot milk to the sugar mixture and mix well. Pour the mixture back into the pan with the remaining hot milk and simmer until thickened, about 3 minutes. Cover the surface with plastic wrap to prevent a crust from forming and set aside.

5. Preheat the oven to 400°F. Remove the plastic wrap and place the pan over low heat. Warm the mixture and add the Cointreau. Beat the 4 remaining egg whites with an electric mixer until soft peaks form. Beat in the remaining 1 tablespoon of sugar. Add one third of the beaten egg whites to the warm soufflé mixture and mix well. Fold in the remaining egg white mixture until no streaks of white show.

6. Place the crepes on a baking sheet covered with parchment paper or sprayed with nonstick vegetable spray. Spoon about ⅓ cup of the soufflé mixture onto each crepe. Fold each crepe in half over the soufflé. Place in the oven and bake until set and lightly browned, about 10 minutes. Serve immediately.

7. To serve, place each crepe on a plate and dust with sifted confectioners' sugar and garnish with a sprig of fresh mint.

MAKES 12 SERVINGS

Each crepe contains approximately: Calories: 186;
Grams of fat: 3; Cholesterol: 38 mg; Sodium: 129 mg

Strawberry Crepe Cakes

2 cups low-fat ricotta cheese
2 tablespoons honey
1 teaspoon pure vanilla extract
1 recipe Cornmeal Crepes (page 189)
4 cups thinly sliced fresh strawberries
16 whole fresh strawberries, fanned
16 fresh mint sprigs

1. Combine the ricotta cheese, honey, and vanilla in a food processor and blend until satin smooth.

2. Spread each crepe with 2 tablespoons of the cheese mixture. Top 4 of the crepes with ¼ cup of the sliced strawberries. Place a second crepe on top of the strawberries, cheese side up, and top the second crepe with ¼ cup strawberries. Repeat twice more until you have 4 crepe cakes.

3. To serve, cut each cake into quarters and garnish with a fanned strawberry and a sprig of mint.

MAKES 16 SERVINGS

Each serving contains approximately: Calories: 111; Grams of fat: 3.5; Cholesterol: 10 mg; Sodium: 186 mg

Puffed Cherry Pancakes

I like to serve these delightfully different sweet pancakes topped with a dollop of either vanilla ice milk or nonfat frozen yogurt. If I am serving them for brunch rather than dessert, I mix the reserved cherry juice I have after draining the cherries with ½ cup of nonfat plain yogurt and serve it as a sauce.

1 tablespoon corn oil margarine

One 16-ounce package frozen unsweetened dark cherries, thawed and
   drained

2 large eggs, separated

¾ cup nonfat milk

½ teaspoon pure vanilla extract

3 tablespoons sugar

¼ teaspoon salt

⅓ cup all-purpose unbleached flour

¾ teaspoon baking powder

1. Preheat the oven to 375°F. Put the margarine in a 10-inch
pie plate and place in the oven just long enough to melt the margarine. Remove from the oven and add the cherries. Return to the
oven and bake the cherries for 10 minutes.

2. While the cherries are baking, beat the egg whites with an
electric mixer until stiff but not dry peaks form and set aside. Combine the egg yolks, milk, and vanilla in a large bowl and mix well.
In another bowl, combine the sugar, salt, flour, and baking powder,
mix well, and add to the milk mixture, stirring just enough to
moisten the dry ingredients. The batter should be lumpy. Fold in
the beaten egg whites. Remove the cherries from the oven and
pour the mixture over the cherries. Return to the oven and bake
until well browned and "puffed," about 20 minutes. Cut into 6 pie-
shaped wedges and serve immediately.

MAKES 6 SERVINGS

*Each serving contains approximately: Calories: 144; Grams of fat: 2.5;
Cholesterol: 71 mg; Sodium: 136 mg*

Cinnamon Crispas

These sweet, crisp, and marvelous-looking flour tortillas are a popular dessert in Mexico. They are also very easy to make!

4 whole-wheat tortillas
4 teaspoons corn oil margarine
2 tablespoons firmly packed light brown sugar
Ground cinnamon for sprinkling

1. Preheat the oven to 400°F. Place the tortillas on a nonstick baking sheet or one sprayed with nonstick vegetable spray.

2. Spread each tortilla with 1 teaspoon of the margarine. Sprinkle the top of each one with 1½ teaspoons of the sugar and a generous amount of cinnamon. Place on the baking sheet and bake until the tortillas have puffed up, are lightly browned, and the sugar has melted and started to bubble, about 8 minutes.

MAKES 4 SERVINGS

Each serving contains approximately: Calories: 177; Grams of fat: 4.8; Cholesterol: 0; Sodium: 249 mg

Blueberry Blintzes

When fresh blueberries are not available, frozen unsweetened berries work well in this recipe.

FOR THE SAUCE
1½ cups nonfat plain yogurt
1½ teaspoons pure vanilla extract
3 tablespoons frozen unsweetened apple juice concentrate

FOR THE FILLING

2 cups low-fat ricotta cheese
2 tablespoons sugar
1½ teaspoons pure vanilla extract
1½ teaspoons fresh lemon juice
1 cup fresh blueberries, picked over and rinsed
1 recipe Crepes (page 187)

1. Preheat the oven to 350°F. Combine the sauce ingredients in a small bowl and mix well. Set aside.

2. In another bowl, combine the cheese, sugar, vanilla, and lemon juice and mix well. Fold in the blueberries, then spoon about 3 tablespoons of the mixture down the center of each crepe and roll the crepe around it. Place each filled crepe, seam side down, on a nonstick baking sheet or one sprayed with nonstick vegetable spray. Bake until lightly browned, about 7 minutes.

3. To serve, spoon 2 tablespoons of the sauce over the top of each blintz.

MAKES 12 SERVINGS

Fruit Blintzes:

Substitute any other fresh berry or fruit for the blueberries in this recipe. If using peaches, add ½ teaspoon of ground cinnamon in step 2.

Each serving contains approximately: Calories: 133; Grams of fat: 3.9; Cholesterol: 31 mg; Sodium: 115 mg

Frozen Desserts

···

You don't have to start from scratch making your ice "cream" to call it your own. Try making some of the recipes that start with vanilla ice milk such as Peanut Butter or Prune and Calvados Ice Milk. I promise you will get raves from your guests. Also, the Watermelon Bombe is a real party conversation piece for children and adults alike and you can surprise and delight your guests at your next "fiesta" by serving them Fire and Ice.

Peanut Butter Ice Milk

···

I love peanut butter and this may be my favorite way to eat it. For a creamy texture use smooth peanut butter and for some crunch, use the nutty variety. For a really unusual dessert, try combining peanut butter ice milk and strawberry jam for a peanut butter and jelly sundae!

1 quart vanilla ice milk, slightly softened
⅓ cup unhomogenized (old-fashioned) peanut butter

Combine the slightly softened ice milk and peanut butter in a large bowl and mix thoroughly. Spoon the mixture back in the carton and place it in the freezer until firm before serving.

MAKES 1 QUART

Each ½-cup serving contains approximately: Calories: 182; Grams of fat: 7.7; Cholesterol: 7 mg; Sodium: 83 mg

Prune and Armagnac Ice Milk

I first tasted an ice cream similar to this in a little bistro in the south of France many years ago. I think you will agree with me that it is truly a winning combination of flavors.

1 quart vanilla ice milk, slightly softened
8 plump, moist, canned pitted prunes (4 ounces), finely chopped
3 tablespoons Armagnac or other brandy

Combine the slightly softened ice milk with the chopped prunes and Armagnac in a bowl and mix thoroughly. Spoon the mixture back into the carton and place it in the freezer until firm before serving.

MAKES 1 QUART

Each ½-cup serving contains approximately: Calories: 165; Grams of fat: 2.4; Cholesterol: 7 mg; Sodium: 82 mg

Homemade Ice "Cream"

There is just nothing like real, homemade ice "cream" and this is an easy and delicious recipe.

4 large egg whites
1/4 cup corn oil
3 cups low-fat milk
2 cups sugar
One 12-ounce can evaporated skim milk, chilled
1 tablespoon pure vanilla extract
1/2 teaspoon salt

1. Combine the egg whites and corn oil in a large, heavy saucepan and blend thoroughly with a whisk. Add the milk and sugar and cook over low heat, stirring constantly, until the mixture begins to coat a metal spoon. Remove from the heat and chill.

2. Add the evaporated milk, vanilla, and salt to the chilled mixture. Blend with a wire whisk and freeze in an ice cream maker according to the manufacturer's instructions.

MAKES 2 QUARTS

Each 1/2-cup serving contains approximately: Calories: 174; Grams of fat: 4; Cholesterol: 4 mg; Sodium: 129 mg

Praline Ice Milk

For a taste of the South in a frozen dessert, try serving this crunchy, easy to make, and sure to please ice milk.

1/4 cup chopped almonds, toasted in a 350°F oven until golden brown, 8 to 10 minutes
1/4 cup sugar
1 pint vanilla ice milk

1. Combine the almonds and sugar in a heavy saucepan and cook over low heat, stirring frequently, until the sugar has completely dissolved and turned a rich golden brown color. Pour the mixture onto a baking sheet generously sprayed with nonstick vegetable spray. Allow to cool and harden. Lift the praline off the baking sheet onto a cutting board and, using a rolling pin, break it into small pieces.

2. Remove the ice milk from the freezer and allow to stand until soft enough to stir in the crushed praline, about 10 minutes. Place the praline ice milk back in the freezer for 15 minutes to harden a bit before spooning into dishes.

MAKES SIX ⅓-CUP SERVINGS

Each serving contains approximately: Calories: 150; Grams of fat: 4.9; Cholesterol: 4 mg; Sodium: 55 mg

Jalapeño Ice Milk

This "hot and cold" dessert is a real conversation piece. I like to serve it with the Cinnamon Crispas on page 198.

1 quart vanilla ice milk
1 teaspoon fresh lime juice
½ teaspoon grated lime rind
1 tablespoon diced jalapeño peppers

Soften the ice milk slightly. Add the remaining ingredients and mix thoroughly. Spoon the mixture back into the container. Return it to the freezer until completely firm before serving.

MAKES 1 QUART

Each ½-cup serving contains approximately: Calories: 114; Grams of fat: 2.3; Cholesterol: 7 mg; Sodium: 82 mg

Pumpkin "Ice Cream"

For a nice change of pace in holiday desserts, try making this easy and delicious frozen dessert. I call it "ice cream," rather than ice milk, which it really is, because it tastes too rich for anyone to question the ingredients.

One 16-ounce can solid pack pumpkin
2 teaspoons ground cinnamon
1 teaspoon ground allspice
¼ teaspoon freshly grated nutmeg
1 quart vanilla ice milk, slightly softened

1. Combine the pumpkin, cinnamon, allspice, and nutmeg in a large bowl or in a food processor and mix well. Add the slightly softened ice milk and blend thoroughly. Spoon the mixture back in the carton and place it in the freezer until firm before serving.

2. Remove the "ice cream" from the freezer about 15 minutes before you plan to serve it, or put the carton in a microwave for 1 minute. This softens it enough so it can be spooned out more easily.

MAKES 1 QUART

Each ½-cup serving contains approximately: Calories: 136; Grams of fat: 2.5; Cholesterol: 7 mg; Sodium: 84 mg

Make-Your-Own Yogurt

This homemade yogurt can be used in any recipe calling for yogurt. If this is more yogurt than you can use in a week's time, reduce the recipe accordingly.

2 cups nonfat dry milk
1 gallon nonfat milk
1 cup low-fat plain yogurt

1. Combine the dry and liquid nonfat milk in a large saucepan and mix thoroughly. Heat slowly for 15 minutes over medium heat. Do not boil.

2. Remove from the heat and allow to cool for 25 minutes. Skim off the film that forms on the surface. Add the yogurt and mix well into the milk mixture.

3. Sterilize a large container (or containers) in boiling water. Pour the mixture into the sterilized container(s) and let them set for 3 to 6 hours. If you have a gas stove, place the container(s) in the oven and the pilot light will keep them at the proper temperature. If you do not have a gas stove, place the container(s) in warm water that you replace or replenish regularly to maintain the temperature.

4. When the mixture has thickened enough to hold together (test it by tilting the container(s) slightly), refrigerate for 4 or 5 hours to thicken to the proper yogurt consistency.

MAKES 4 QUARTS

Vanilla Yogurt:

Add ½ cup sugar and ¼ cup pure vanilla extract in step 3. To make only 1 cup of vanilla yogurt, add 1½ teaspoons sugar and ¾ teaspoon vanilla extract to 1 cup of the prepared yogurt. If you use 1 cup commercial nonfat yogurt, add exactly the same amount of sugar and vanilla extract.

Each 1-cup serving contains approximately: Calories: 147; Grams of fat: negligible; Cholesterol: 8 mg; Sodium: 218 mg

Fast Frozen Yogurt

Because this yogurt has never actually been frozen, all of the valuable bacteria in it are still alive. You will find that this delicious and creamy dessert is also a great deal less expensive when you make it yourself. Serve it immediately for a frozen dessert. Refrigerate any leftover in a covered container to serve later as a custard.

1 envelope unflavored gelatin
2 tablespoons cold water
¼ cup boiling water
1 cup nonfat plain yogurt
¼ cup nonfat dry milk
¼ cup sugar
1½ teaspoons pure vanilla extract
2 cups crushed ice

1. Soften the gelatin in the cold water and allow to stand for 5 minutes. Add the boiling water and stir until the gelatin is completely dissolved. Combine the gelatin-water mixture with the yogurt and mix well. Refrigerate until firmly jelled, about 2 hours.

2. Combine the jelled yogurt, dry milk, sugar, vanilla, and crushed ice in a blender and blend until smooth.

MAKES SIX ½-CUP SERVINGS

Each serving contains approximately: Calories: 76;
Grams of fat: negligible; Cholesterol: 2 mg; Sodium: 57 mg

Strawberry Frozen Yogurt

This is a refreshing dessert served by itself or accompanied with a selection of other berries or fresh fruits.

2 cups fresh strawberries, hulled
½ cup confectioners' sugar
1 tablespoon fresh lemon juice
3 cups nonfat plain yogurt

1. Combine the strawberries, sugar, and lemon juice in a blender and puree. Add the yogurt and blend until thoroughly mixed. Pour the mixture into a shallow bowl and place in the coldest part of the freezer so that it will freeze as fast as possible, about 2 hours.

2. If the mixture is too hard, allow to stand until soft enough to spoon into bowls or sherbet glasses.

MAKES EIGHT ½-CUP SERVINGS

Each serving contains approximately: Calories: 87; Grams of fat: negligible; Cholesterol: 2 mg; Sodium: 66 mg

Frozen Chocolate Yogurt

2 cups low-fat milk
½ cup nonfat liquid egg substitute
¾ cup sugar
⅓ cup canola oil
¾ cup unsweetened cocoa powder
1½ teaspoons pure vanilla extract
2 cups nonfat plain yogurt

1. In a medium-size nonaluminum saucepan, bring the milk almost to boiling. Remove from the heat and set aside. In a bowl, beat the egg substitute with the sugar and oil until thickened. Gradually beat in the hot milk.

2. Pour the mixture back into the saucepan and cook over medium-low heat, stirring constantly with a wooden spoon, until the mixture thickens enough to lightly coat the spoon, 15 to 20 minutes. Do not allow the mixture to boil or it will curdle.

3. Stir the cocoa and vanilla into the custard. Strain the mixture through a fine sieve into a large bowl. Let cool to room temperature. Whisk the yogurt until smooth in another bowl, then whisk the yogurt into the cooled custard, mixing thoroughly. Freeze according to the manufacturer's directions in a 2-quart or larger ice-cream freezer.

MAKES 1½ QUARTS; TWELVE ½-CUP SERVINGS

Each serving contains approximately: Calories: 170; Grams of fat: 8; Cholesterol: 4 mg; Sodium: 69 mg

Fat-Free Frozen Fruit Custard

Any sliced or chopped frozen fruit may be used in this recipe. If you prefer, you may use chilled rather than frozen fruit, and use this custard as a sauce for other fruits, cakes, or puddings.

1 envelope unflavored gelatin
2 tablespoons cool water
¼ cup boiling water
1 cup nonfat cottage cheese
¼ cup nonfat dry milk
3 tablespoons sugar
1½ teaspoons pure vanilla extract
2 teaspoons fresh lemon juice
¼ cup ice water
1½ cups frozen fresh fruit

1. Soften the gelatin in the cool water. Add the boiling water and stir until the gelatin is completely dissolved. Pour the gelatin mixture into a blender and add the cottage cheese, dry milk, sugar, vanilla, and lemon juice. Blend until completely smooth. Pour the mixture into a bowl, cover, and refrigerate until firm.

2. Pour the ice water into the blender, then add the cottage cheese mixture and frozen fruit and blend until smooth. Serve immediately.

MAKES SIX ½-CUP SERVINGS

Each serving contains approximately: Calories: 94; Grams of fat: negligible; Cholesterol: 4 mg; Sodium: 186 mg

Cinnamon Gelato

This is a wonderfully refreshing and unusual dessert. It is particularly nice served after a very spicy meal.

½ teaspoon unflavored gelatin
1 tablespoon cool water
1¼ cups whole milk
One 12-ounce can evaporated skim milk
3 tablespoon light corn syrup
⅓ cup nonfat dry milk
½ cup sugar
1 tablespoon ground cinnamon

1. Soften the gelatin in the water and set aside.

2. Combine the milk, evaporated milk, and corn syrup in a saucepan. Combine the dry milk, sugar, and cinnamon in a bowl, mix well, and add to the saucepan. Slowly bring to a simmer, not a full boil. Remove from the heat and stir in the softened gelatin. Allow to cool to room temperature and then freeze in an ice cream maker according to the manufacturer's instructions.

MAKES SIX ½-CUP SERVINGS

Each serving contains approximately: Calories: 206; Grams of fat: 2.3; Cholesterol: 9 mg; Sodium: 143 mg

Pear Sherbet

This delicately flavored frozen dessert is best made the day it is to be served.

6 ripe pears, peeled, cored, and halved
4 cups water
½ cup sugar

1. Combine all the ingredients in a large saucepan and bring to a boil. Reduce the heat to low, cover, and cook until the pears are soft, about 20 minutes. At this point the liquid should be reduced by half. If not, remove the pears from the liquid and continue to simmer the liquid until it is reduced by half. Put the pears and cooking liquid in a blender and blend until completely smooth.

2. Pour the mixture in a large bowl and place in the freezer. Every half hour, beat the mixture well using a wire whisk. Repeat this procedure six times. After whipping for the last time, cover tightly or the pear sherbet will lose much of its flavor.

MAKES EIGHT ½-CUP SERVINGS

Each serving contains approximately: Calories: 131;
Grams of fat: negligible; Cholesterol: 0; Sodium: negligible

Peachy Gravita

For a really light and totally refreshing dessert, try serving this Peachy Gravita after your next dinner party.

2 large peaches, peeled, pitted, and diced
½ cup sweet marsala
½ cup fresh orange juice
2 large egg whites

1. Combine the peaches, marsala, and orange juice in a medium-size saucepan and bring to a boil. Reduce the heat to low and simmer for 5 minutes. Remove from the heat and allow to cool to room temperature. Spoon the mixture into a blender and puree. Strain the puree through a fine-mesh strainer or sieve and pour in a shallow bowl. Place the bowl in the freezer and freeze until just slushy around the edges, about 30 minutes.

2. Remove from the freezer and stir to break up the ice crystals. Beat the egg whites with an electric mixer until stiff but not dry peaks form, then fold them into the peach mixture until no streaks of white show. Return to the freezer and freeze until firm, about 2 hours.

MAKES SIX ½-CUP SERVINGS

Each serving contains approximately: Calories: 62;
Grams of fat: negligible; Cholesterol: 0; Sodium: 20 mg

Lemon Frost

This is a very light and refreshing dessert but it should not be made more than one day ahead of the time you plan to serve it, as it tends to lose its flavor.

> 1 large egg white
> ⅓ cup water
> ⅓ cup nonfat dry milk
> 1 large egg yolk, slightly beaten
> ⅓ cup sugar
> ¼ teaspoon grated lemon rind
> 3 tablespoons fresh lemon juice
> Dash salt

1. Combine the egg white, water, and dry milk in a large bowl. Beat with an electric mixer until stiff peaks form. In another bowl, mix the remaining ingredients, then gradually beat them into the whipped egg white and milk.

2. Spoon the mixture into six ramekins or custard cups and freeze. Serve within 2 days or it tends to lose its flavor.

MAKES 6 SERVINGS

Lime Frost:

Substitute grated lime peel and fresh lime juice for the lemon peel and juice called for in the recipe.

Orange Frost:

Substitute grated orange peel and fresh orange juice for the lemon peel and juice.

Each serving contains approximately: Calories: 83;
Grams of fat: negligible; Cholesterol: 35 mg; Sodium: 111 mg

Irish Cream Sundae

Here is a fabulous dessert for a big backyard barbecue. It is a classic ice cream sundae with an unusual taste twist that is truly delicious.

2 quarts nonfat frozen vanilla yogurt

FOR THE SAUCE (MAKES 2 CUPS)
One 12-ounce can evaporated skim milk
½ cup nonfat milk
2 tablespoons cornstarch
1 tablespoon roasted carob powder (available in health food stores)
1 tablespoon decaffeinated instant coffee granules
3 tablespoons sugar
2 teaspoons pure vanilla extract
¼ teaspoon pure almond extract

1. To make the sauce, combine the milks and cornstarch in a small saucepan and mix until the cornstarch is completely dissolved. Add the carob powder, instant coffee, and sugar, mix well, and cook over medium heat, stirring constantly, until it comes to a boil. Continue to boil for 1 minute.

2. Remove from the heat and add the extracts. Mix well and set aside to cool to room temperature. *Do not refrigerate.*

3. To serve, spoon 2 tablespoons of the sauce over ½ cup of frozen yogurt.

MAKES 16 SERVINGS

Each serving (including sauce) contains approximately: Calories: 114;
Grams of fat: negligible; Cholesterol: 1 mg; Sodium: 122 mg

Each 2 tablespoons of sauce contains approximately: Calories: 34;
Grams of fat: negligible; Cholesterol: 1 mg; Sodium: 32 mg

Hot Caramel Sundae

For all of the people who prefer caramel or butterscotch to chocolate, this is a fabulous alternative to the hot fudge sundae. This sauce is also delicious on cakes and puddings.

1 quart vanilla ice milk

FOR THE CARAMEL SAUCE (MAKES 1½ CUPS)
One 12-ounce can evaporated skim milk
1 tablespoon cornstarch
2 tablespoons corn oil margarine
½ cup firmly packed dark brown sugar
1 teaspoon pure vanilla extract

1. To make the sauce, combine the milk and cornstarch in a heavy saucepan and mix until the cornstarch is completely dissolved. Add the margarine and brown sugar and cook over medium heat, stirring constantly with a wire whisk, until the mixture comes to a boil and starts to thicken. Remove from the heat and stir in the vanilla.

2. To make the sundaes, spoon ½ cup of the ice milk into each of eight bowls and top with 3 tablespoons of the sauce.

MAKES 8 SERVINGS

Each serving contains approximately: Calories: 335; Grams of fat: 9.2; Cholesterol: 10 mg; Sodium: 205 mg

1 tablespoon of sauce contains approximately: Calories: 73; Grams of fat: 2.3; Cholesterol: 1 mg; Sodium: 41 mg

Hot Fudge Sundae

The story of how this popular dessert was created has always fascinated me. The legend is that there was once a very spoiled little prince who always got everything he asked for. Eventually he had a great deal of trouble trying to think of new things to ask for, so he would sit for hours just saying, "I want . . . I want . . . I want . . ." and then one day he said, "I want a dessert that is both hot and cold at the same time." His newest request was immediately sent to the king's personal chef, and the clever fellow invented the hot fudge sundae. Now I have taken this much-loved recipe and lowered the calories and fat as much as possible without destroying the basic integrity of this "royal" dessert.

1 quart vanilla ice milk

For the chocolate fudge sauce (makes 1½ cups)
2 tablespoons corn oil margarine
½ cup unsweetened cocoa powder, sifted
One 12-ounce can evaporated skim milk, heated to the boiling point
½ cup sugar
½ teaspoon ground cinnamon
1 teaspoon pure vanilla extract

1. To make the sauce, melt the margarine over medium-low heat. Add the cocoa powder and cook, over low heat, for 2 minutes, stirring constantly. Add the hot milk, stirring constantly with a wire whisk. Add the sugar and cinnamon and continue to simmer, stirring constantly, until thickened. Remove from the heat and stir in the vanilla.

2. To make the sundaes, spoon ½ cup of the ice milk into each of eight dishes and top each serving with 3 tablespoons of the hot fudge sauce.

Makes 8 servings

Each serving contains approximately: Calories: 313; Grams of fat: 8.7; Cholesterol: 5 mg; Sodium: 211 mg

1 tablespoon of sauce contains approximately: Calories: 61; Grams of fat: 1.7; Cholesterol: 1 mg; Sodium: 41 mg

Strawberry Parfait

If you don't have parfait glasses for serving this dessert, then either use regular glasses or serve it as a sundae, using a bowl and spooning all of the sauce over the top of the ice milk. This strawberry sauce is also delicious as a jam on toast, pancakes, and waffles and a tasty topping for cereal and yogurt.

FOR THE SAUCE

*1 pound fresh or thawed frozen unsweetened strawberries, hulled and
    chopped*
2 tablespoons sugar

TO COMPLETE THE SUNDAE

1 pint vanilla ice milk
Fresh mint sprigs for garnish (optional)

1. To make the sauce, put half the chopped strawberries and the sugar in a blender and puree. Combine the puree and the remaining chopped strawberries and mix well. Cover and refrigerate until cold.

2. To make each parfait, spoon ¼ cup of the ice milk into the bottom of a parfait glass. Top with 2 tablespoons of the strawberry sauce. Spoon another ¼ cup of the ice milk on top of the sauce and top with another 2 tablespoons of the sauce. Garnish with a sprig of fresh mint, if desired.

MAKES 4 SERVINGS

*Each serving contains approximately: Calories: 183; Grams of fat: 2.4;
Cholesterol: 7 mg; Sodium: 84 mg*

Banana Split

Just the name says it all about this classic soda fountain extravaganza. However, my version of this famous American favorite is definitely lighter than you will find in most neighborhood ice cream parlors!

16 almonds, chopped (2 tablespoons)
12 scoops (3 cups) vanilla ice milk
3 small bananas
1½ cups Chocolate Sauce (page 218)
1½ cups Strawberry Topping (page 218)
6 fresh strawberries, halved (optional)

1. Preheat the oven to 350°F. Toast the almonds on a baking sheet until golden brown, 8 to 10 minutes. Watch carefully since they burn easily. Set aside.

2. Place 2 scoops of ice milk in each of six banana-split dishes. Slice each banana in quarters lengthwise. Place a banana quarter on each side of each dish.

3. Pour ¼ cup of the chocolate sauce over one of the scoops of ice milk in each of the dishes. Pour ¼ cup of the strawberry topping over each of the remaining scoops of ice milk. Sprinkle 1 teaspoon of the toasted almonds over the top of each banana split. Place a strawberry half on top of each scoop of ice milk, if desired.

MAKES 6 SERVINGS

Each serving contains approximately: Calories: 372; Grams of fat: 10;
Cholesterol: 10 mg; Sodium: 137 mg

Chocolate Sauce

1½ cups nonfat milk
2 tablespoons corn oil margarine
½ cup unsweetened cocoa powder
¾ cup sugar

1. In a saucepan over medium heat, scald the milk, heating it until bubbles begin to form around the edges of the pan. In another saucepan over medium heat, melt the margarine. Add the cocoa to the margarine, mix thoroughly, and cook about 3 minutes, being careful not to burn.

2. Remove the cocoa mixture from the heat and add the scalded milk all at once, rapidly stirring with a wire whisk. Add the sugar, return the mixture to medium heat, and simmer, stirring with a whisk, until the sauce reaches the desired thickness.

MAKES 1 ½ CUPS; SIX ¼-CUP SERVINGS

Each serving contains approximately: Calories: 175; Grams of fat: 6; Cholesterol: 1 mg; Sodium: 84 mg

Strawberry Topping

2 cups fresh or frozen unsweetened strawberries, thawed
1 teaspoon fresh lemon juice
⅓ cup sugar
½ cup water
1 tablespoon arrowroot

1. In a heavy saucepan over very low heat, cook the berries, covered, for about 10 minutes. Uncover, bring to a boil, and boil for 1 minute. Remove from the heat, add the lemon juice and sugar, and mix well.

2. Combine the water and arrowroot in a small saucepan and bring to a boil. Simmer until the mixture is clear and slightly thick-

ened, about 2 minutes. Remove from the heat and allow the mixture to cool to room temperature.

3. Add the arrowroot mixture to the berries and blend well. Allow the topping to cool to room temperature and store in the refrigerator for up to 2 weeks.

MAKES 2 CUPS; EIGHT ¼-CUP SERVINGS

Each serving contains approximately: Calories: 47; Grams of fat: negligible; Cholesterol: negligible; Sodium: 1 mg

Peach Melba

This classic dessert is still one of my own favorite flavor combinations. I like it even better with a little Grand Marnier in the raspberry sauce. You can substitute ice milk for the frozen yogurt called for in the recipe but I prefer the slight tanginess of the yogurt.

6 large, ripe peaches, thoroughly washed
¼ cup plus 2 tablespoons sugar
2 teaspoons pure vanilla extract
One 12-ounce package frozen unsweetened raspberries, thawed
1 tablespoon fresh lemon juice
1 tablespoon Grand Marnier or other orange-flavored liqueur
1 pint nonfat vanilla frozen yogurt

1. Place the clean peaches in a saucepan and cover with water. Add 2 tablespoons of the sugar and the vanilla. Slowly bring to a boil over medium heat. Reduce the heat to low and simmer, covered, for 10 minutes. Drain the peaches and cool till safe enough to handle. Remove the skins and cut into halves, discarding the pits. Set aside.

2. Put the raspberries, the remaining ¼ cup sugar, and the lemon juice in a blender and puree. Strain the puree through a fine-mesh strainer or sieve into a bowl to remove the seeds. Stir in the Grand Marnier.

3. To serve, place a ⅓-cup scoop of the frozen yogurt in each of six bowls or sherbet glasses. Top each scoop of yogurt with a peach half, cut side down. Spoon ¼ cup of the raspberry sauce over each serving.

MAKES 6 SERVINGS

Each serving contains approximately: Calories: 247;
Grams of fat: negligible; Cholesterol: negligible; Sodium: 65 mg

Fire and Ice

This whimsical Southwestern dessert is designed to represent all the colors of the Mexican flag. I developed it for an easy, make-ahead casual party menu for *Cooking Healthy* magazine. It is a perfect finale for any fiesta and it's fun to decorate each serving with a little Mexican flag sticking out of the top.

> 1 cup water
> ¼ cup sugar
> ½ teaspoon grated lime rind
> 4 kiwis, peeled and chopped (1 cup)
> 1 tablespoon fresh lime juice
> ½ recipe Jalapeño Ice Milk (page 204)
> 1 cup fresh raspberries

1. Combine the water, sugar, and lime rind in a small saucepan and bring to a boil. Boil, uncovered, for 5 minutes. It will reduce by about one third. Remove from the heat and cool to room temperature.

2. Combine the chopped kiwis and lime juice in a blender and puree. Add the water mixture and pour through a fine strainer to remove the kiwi seeds and lime peel, pressing all of the liquid through the strainer with the back of a spoon. Refrigerate the strained puree until cold.

3. Pour ¼ cup of the kiwi puree into each of six chilled bowls. Scoop ⅓ cup of the jalapeño ice milk in the center of each bowl. Sprinkle the raspberries around the ice milk on top of the puree.

MAKES 6 SERVINGS

Each serving contains approximately: Calories: 190; Grams of fat: 1.8; Cholesterol: 4 mg; Sodium: 72 mg

Cinnamon Apple Raisin Frozen Trifle

This is a fabulous make-ahead dessert for parties of all types. For an even more indulgent dish, serve it with the warm Caramel Sauce on page 214!

½ cup unsweetened apple juice
½ cup dark raisins
2 teaspoons ground cinnamon
4 large Golden Delicious apples, peeled, cored, and finely diced (4 cups)
One 8-ounce angel food cake, cut into 1-inch cubes (4 cups)
¼ cup Calvados or brandy
3 cups nonfat vanilla frozen yogurt

1. Combine the apple juice, raisins, and cinnamon in a skillet and bring to a boil. Add the apples and cook, stirring frequently, until they can easily be pierced with a fork and all of the liquid has been absorbed. Remove from the heat, cool to room temperature, and refrigerate until cold before proceeding.

2. To assemble the trifle, place one third of the cake in the bottom of a bowl or trifle dish. Sprinkle it with one third of the Calvados. Spoon 1 cup of the frozen yogurt evenly over the cake. Spoon one third of the chilled apple mixture evenly over the top.

Repeat the same layering process twice. Cover the bowl or dish tightly with plastic wrap and place in the freezer until firm.

3. Remove the frozen trifle from the freezer about 15 minutes before you plan to serve it so that it can soften a bit and more easily be spooned out of the dish.

MAKES 12 SERVINGS

Each serving contains approximately: Calories: 202;
Grams of fat: negligible; Cholesterol: 0; Sodium: 103 mg

Neapolitan Bombe

If you're looking for an easy-to-make party dessert with plenty of pizzazz, this tricolored bombe is perfect. A bombe is a traditional frozen dessert made of at least two kinds of ice cream or sherbet layered in a mold and then unmolded and sliced like a cake. Bombes are usually made in a tall, round-bottomed mold so that when unmolded the shape is like that of a round-topped mountain. However, you can make a bombe in any shape mold you desire.

1½ quarts strawberry ice milk
1 quart vanilla ice milk
1 pint chocolate ice milk

1. Line an 8-cup mold with plastic wrap. Soften the strawberry ice milk slightly, then spread it in an even layer, about 1½ inches thick, on the inner surface of the mold. Cover the top surface with plastic wrap and place it in the freezer until it's hard.

2. Soften the vanilla ice milk slightly. Remove the mold from the freezer and remove the plastic wrap covering the surface. Spread the vanilla ice milk on top of the strawberry ice milk in an even layer about 1½ inches thick. Again cover the top with plastic wrap and place the bombe back in the freezer until hard.

3. Soften the chocolate ice milk slightly. Remove the bombe from the freezer and remove the plastic wrap on the top. Fill the

center cavity with the chocolate ice milk and smooth the top surface with a spatula. Cover the top with plastic wrap and place the bombe back in the freezer until hard.

4. To serve, uncover the top of the bombe and turn it out onto a large serving plate. Peel off the plastic wrap and smooth out any wrinkle lines using a spatula or a knife. Cut like a cake into 16 pie-shaped, striped slices. Serve at once.

MAKES 16 SERVINGS

Each serving contains approximately: Calories: 151; Grams of fat: 4; Cholesterol: 12 mg; Sodium: 93 mg

Watermelon Bombe

1 quart lime sherbet
1 pint pineapple sherbet
1 cup raspberry sherbet
2 tablespoons mini chocolate chips

1. Line an 8-cup mold or bowl with plastic wrap or aluminum foil. Soften the lime sherbet slightly and spread it in an even layer, about 1½ inches thick, over the inner surface of the mold. Cover the surface of the sherbet with plastic wrap and place it in the freezer until hard.

2. Soften the pineapple sherbet slightly. Remove the mold from the freezer and remove the plastic wrap from the lime sherbet. Spread the softened pineapple sherbet on top of the lime sherbet in an even layer about 1½ inches thick. Cover again and return to the freezer to harden.

3. Soften the raspberry sherbet slightly and stir in the chocolate chips. Remove the bombe from the freezer and remove the plastic wrap. Fill the center cavity with the chocolate-studded sherbet and smooth the top with a spatula. Cover with plastic wrap and return to the freezer to harden.

4. To serve, remove the plastic wrap and turn the bombe onto a serving plate. Peel off the plastic wrap or foil covering the surface and smooth out any wrinkle lines using a spatula or knife. Cut like a cake into 16 pie-shaped wedges. Serve at once.

MAKES 16 SERVINGS

Each serving contains approximately: Calories: 127; Grams of fat: 2.2; Cholesterol: 6 mg; Sodium: 39 mg

Vanilla Ice Milk Crepes with Caramel Sauce

This is a wonderful dessert for entertaining because everything but the sauce can be made several days ahead of time. The crepes may be filled with the ice milk and frozen in a single layer in a covered dish or pan. (Be sure to cover them tightly or the ice milk will pick up the flavors or other foods in the freezer.) Then, before your guests arrive, make the sauce and set it aside, covered, at room temperature until you are ready to use it. Remove the frozen crepes from the freezer about 10 minutes before serving to allow them to soften slightly.

1 recipe Crepes (page 187)
3 cups vanilla ice milk, slightly softened
1½ cups Caramel Sauce (page 214)

1. Fill each crepe with ¼ cup of the ice milk. Fold the crepe around the ice milk and place, seam side down, in a single layer in a dish or pan. Cover tightly and place in the freezer until ready to serve.

2. To serve, place each frozen crepe on a plate and allow to soften slightly. (If serving the sauce hot, it is not necessary for the frozen crepes to soften.) Top each crepe with 2 tablespoons of the sauce.

MAKES 12 SERVINGS

Chocolate Ice Milk Crepes with Caramel Rum Sauce:

Substitute chocolate ice milk for the vanilla ice milk and add 1 table-spoon dark rum to the caramel sauce when you add the vanilla extract.

Each serving contains approximately: Calories: 158; Grams of fat: 4.4;
Cholesterol: 25 mg; Sodium: 106 mg

Ice Cream Cake

This is a quick, easy, and inexpensive dessert. It is ideal for children's birthday parties because the classic combination of ice cream and cake is already combined.

One 18½-ounce box any flavor light cake mix, prepared according to
  package directions in two 8- or 9-inch round cake pans and cooled
1 quart any flavor ice milk, slightly softened
2 cups light whipped topping

1. Place 1 cake layer on a serving plate. Cover evenly with the ice milk and top with the second cake layer. Freeze several hours, until the ice milk is firm. Frost the sides and top of the cake with the whipped topping and return to the freezer for at least 1 hour.

2. Remove the cake from the freezer 5 minutes before slicing.

MAKES 12 SERVINGS

Each serving contains approximately: Calories: 265;
Grams of fat: 5; Cholesterol: 42 mg; Sodium: 346 mg

Ice Cream Roll

4 large egg whites, at room temperature
¼ teaspoon cream of tartar
½ cup sugar
½ cup nonfat liquid egg substitute
1 teaspoon fresh lemon juice
2 tablespoons water
½ cup all-purpose unbleached flour
2 tablespoons confectioners' sugar
1 quart chocolate ice milk, softened

1. Preheat the oven to 350°F. Spray a 15½ x 10½-inch baking sheet with nonstick vegetable spray. Line the bottom with waxed paper and spray the paper. Set aside.

2. In a large bowl, beat the egg whites and cream of tartar with an electric mixer until soft peaks form. Gradually beat in ¼ cup of the sugar until the peaks are stiff but not dry.

3. In a medium-size bowl, beat the egg substitute slightly, then gradually beat in the remaining ¼ cup sugar, the lemon juice, and water. Fold into the egg whites and then fold in the flour. Spread evenly in the prepared baking sheet. Bake until the cake springs back when lightly touched, about 15 minutes. Do not overbake.

4. Lay a clean towel on a flat surface. Dust with the confectioners' sugar. When the cake is baked, immediately turn it out onto the prepared towel and remove the waxed paper. Carefully roll up the warm cake and towel from the narrow end of the cake.

5. When the cake is cool, carefully unroll and remove the towel. Spread the ice milk evenly over the cake, reroll, and wrap in aluminum foil. Freeze until very firm before slicing, at least 6 hours. Cut into 10 slices to serve.

MAKES 10 SERVINGS

Variation:

Use any other type of ice milk, sherbet, sorbet, or frozen yogurt to change the flavor.

Each serving contains approximately: Calories: 168; Grams of fat: 3; Cholesterol: 7 mg; Sodium: 94 mg

Baked Alaska

....

To make this already impressive dessert even more impressive, you can pour a little brandy over the top of it and flame it at the table.

One 9-inch light yellow cake layer
1 quart vanilla ice milk
1 quart raspberry sorbet
4 large egg whites
½ teaspoon cream of tartar
½ cup sugar

1. Place the cake on a large baking sheet and put it in the freezer to chill. Line a 1½-quart mixing bowl with aluminum foil. Pack the ice milk along the bottom and sides of it. Fill the center with the sorbet. Place a piece of waxed paper on top and press down to pack it firmly. Freeze until firm.

2. Invert the ice milk-sorbet bowl on top of the cake layer and peel off the foil. The cake will probably extend about ½ inch beyond the ice milk. Place it back in the freezer while making the meringue. Preheat the oven to 450°F.

3. In a large bowl, beat the egg whites and cream of tartar with an electric mixer until soft peaks form. Gradually beat in the sugar until stiff peaks form. Remove the cake from the freezer and quickly spread the meringue over the cake and ice milk, covering it

completely. Seal the meringue to the baking sheet so that none of the cake or ice milk is exposed.

4. Bake the cake until the meringue is lightly browned, 4 to 5 minutes. Cut into wedges and serve immediately.

MAKES 12 SERVINGS

Each serving contains approximately: Calories: 274; Grams of fat: 2.9; Cholesterol: 6 mg; Sodium: 210 mg

Quick and Easy Bite-Size Ice Cream Sandwiches

1 pint vanilla ice milk
1 teaspoon pure vanilla extract
1 package chocolate wafer cookies

1. Soften the ice milk in a small bowl for 3 minutes, then stir in the vanilla. Working quickly, spread about 1½ tablespoons of ice milk on half the chocolate wafers, topping each with another wafer.

2. Immediately place each sandwich on a flat pan in the freezer since the ice milk melts rapidly. When frozen, the sandwiches may be stored in plastic bags or containers. They will keep for 2 weeks.

MAKES ABOUT 20 SANDWICHES

Variation:

Stir 2 tablespoons chunk-style peanut butter into the ice milk along with the vanilla.

Each sandwich contains approximately: Calories: 27; Grams of fat: negligible; Cholesterol: 2 mg; Sodium: 18 mg

Candies and Condiments

The recipes in this section are most often simply lighter versions of higher calorie sweets rather than truly "light." It is virtually impossible to make candy and snacks really low-fat, so my goal in this category was to make them as healthy as possible and, of course, tasty and satisfying at the same time!

Almond Meringue Drops

These light and crunchy little morsels are a wonderful substitute for higher calories candies. You can even make them in assorted pastel colors and they look very much like bonbons.

1 cup sliced blanched almonds (4½ ounces)
4 large egg whites
½ teaspoon cream of tartar
½ cup sugar

1. Preheat the oven to 350°F. Spread the almonds on a baking sheet and toast until they are golden brown, 8 to 10 minutes. Watch them carefully as they burn easily. Set aside to cool.

2. Beat the egg whites in a large bowl with an electric mixer until frothy. Add the cream of tartar and beat until soft peaks form. Slowly add the sugar and beat until stiff peaks form. Carefully fold in the toasted almonds.

3. Drop the mixture by teaspoonsful onto a baking sheet lined with parchment paper. Bake until lightly browned, about 12 minutes. Allow to cool to room temperature and then "peel" them off the paper. They can be stored, tightly covered, at room temperature or refrigerated for 2 weeks.

MAKES 48 DROPS

Each drop contains approximately: Calories: 28; Grams of fat: 1.5; Cholesterol: 0; Sodium: 7 mg

Candied Pecans

Last Christmas my daughter-in-law made these habit-forming sweet nuts as gifts for her friends and family. I liked them so much I asked her for the recipe so that I could share it with my readers.

1 teaspoon cold water
1 large egg white
2 cups large pecan halves
½ cup sugar
1 teaspoon ground cinnamon
1 teaspoon salt

1. Preheat the oven to 225°F. Beat the water and egg white together until frothy, then stir in the pecans. Combine the sugar, cinnamon, and salt. Mix well and add to the pecans.

2. Spread the mixture out on a baking sheet and bake, stirring occasionally, until well browned, about 1½ hours.

3. Remove from the oven and before allowing to cool completely, make sure that the pecans are all separated from each other. Store in an airtight container. They will keep for a few weeks, but are best during the first week.

MAKES 2 ⅔ CUPS

Each 2-tablespoon serving contains approximately: Calories: 89;
Grams of fat: 7; Cholesterol: 0; Sodium: 115 mg

Chewy Almond Popcorn Balls

1 cup chopped almonds
½ cup water
1½ cups sugar
1 tablespoon cider vinegar
½ teaspoon ground cinnamon
¼ teaspoon salt
2 teaspoons pure vanilla extract
12 cups popped popcorn (made from ½ cup popcorn kernels)

1. Preheat the oven to 350°F. Place the chopped almonds on a baking sheet and toast in the oven until golden brown, 8 to 10 minutes. Watch them carefully as they burn easily. Set aside.

2. Combine the water, sugar, vinegar, cinnamon, and salt in a large saucepan. Cook slowly over medium-low heat, stirring occasionally, until a little of the mixture dropped into cold water forms a hard ball (250°F on a candy thermometer). Remove the mixture from the heat and stir in the vanilla.

3. Combine the popcorn and toasted almonds and slowly pour the liquid over the popcorn-almond mixture, tossing it continuously until it is cool enough to handle. Grease your hands lightly with

corn oil margarine. Quickly shape the popcorn mixture into eighteen 3-inch balls, pressing each ball firmly so it will hold its shape.

4. Wrap each ball individually in either plastic wrap, waxed paper, or aluminum foil or place each ball in a small plastic bag and seal with a twist-tie. They will keep about 1 week.

MAKES 18 POPCORN BALLS

Each ball contains approximately: Calories: 132; Grams of fat: 4.3; Cholesterol: 0; Sodium: 34 mg

Peanut Clusters

It is easier to form the balls for these peanut clusters if you oil your hands slightly so that the mixture doesn't stick to your fingers.

⅓ cup honey
2 large egg whites
½ teaspoon ground cinnamon
¼ teaspoon salt
1½ cups quick-cooking rolled oats
½ cup chopped peanuts

1. Preheat the oven to 350°F. Combine the honey, egg whites, cinnamon, and salt in a large bowl and mix well. Add the oats and peanuts and mix until thoroughly combined.

2. Form the mixture into 24 compact little walnut-size balls and place them on a nonstick baking sheet or one that has been lined with parchment paper or sprayed with nonstick vegetable spray. Bake until lightly browned, about 12 minutes.

MAKES 24 CLUSTERS

Each cluster contains approximately: Calories: 47; Grams of fat: 1.8; Cholesterol: 0; Sodium: 43 mg

Spiced Walnuts

These tasty treats make wonderful gifts for holiday giving. They are also a much appreciated host or hostess gift anytime of the year.

½ cup sugar
½ cup cornstarch
4 teaspoons ground cinnamon
1 teaspoon ground allspice
⅔ teaspoon freshly grated nutmeg
¼ teaspoon ground ginger
2 large egg whites
2 cups walnut halves

1. Preheat the oven to 250°F. In a small bowl sift together the sugar, cornstarch, and spices. Mix well and set aside.

2. In a medium-size bowl, lightly beat the egg whites. Add the walnuts and mix well. Dip each walnut in the spice mixture to coat, and shake off any excess. Arrange, well-spaced, on a nonstick baking sheet, or one lined with parchment paper or sprayed with nonstick vegetable spray. Bake until they are lightly browned, about 1½ hours. Remove the walnuts from the oven and allow to cool on the pan. Store in a tightly covered container. They will keep frozen for 1 month or 2 weeks in the refrigerator.

MAKES 2 CUPS; SIXTEEN 2-TABLESPOON SERVINGS

Each serving contains approximately: Calories: 140; Grams of fat: 9; Cholesterol: 0; Sodium: 7 mg

Sweet Garbanzo Nuts

If you're looking for a lower calorie alternative to honey-roasted peanuts, or any other higher calorie snack, try making these tasty and very satisfying garbanzo nuts. You can control the amount of crunchiness you want by the length of time you bake them in the oven. Also, you can adjust the sweetness level and the spices to suit your own taste.

Two 15½-ounce cans garbanzo beans (chick-peas), drained
½ cup sugar
1 tablespoon ground cinnamon
1½ teaspoons ground allspice
Freshly grated nutmeg for sprinkling

1. Put the drained garbanzo beans in a saucepan with enough water to cover by 1 inch. Add the sugar, cinnamon, and allspice and bring to a boil over medium heat. Reduce the heat to low and simmer for 30 minutes. Remove from the heat and allow to cool to room temperature.

2. Preheat the oven to 375°F. Drain the cooled beans thoroughly. Put them in a 9 x 13-inch baking pan sprayed with nonstick vegetable spray and then spray the beans with the nonstick spray. Sprinkle with nutmeg. Bake until the beans are browned and crisp, about 1 hour. Stir occasionally while baking for more even browning.

MAKES EIGHT ¼-CUP SERVINGS

Each serving contains approximately: Calories: 182; Grams of fat: 1.3;
Cholesterol: 0; Sodium: 329 mg

Granola

This granola has a truly interesting taste and texture because it contains so many different ingredients. However, you don't have to include every ingredient called for in the recipe. For instance, if you don't have any pine nuts, just use 2 tablespoons of some other nut.

1½ cups quick-cooking rolled oats
1 tablespoon chopped almonds
1 tablespoon chopped walnuts
1 tablespoon chopped pecans
1 tablespoon pine nuts
1 tablespoon shelled sunflower seeds
½ teaspoon ground cinnamon
¼ teaspoon ground cloves
¼ teaspoon freshly grated nutmeg
1 teaspoon honey
2 teaspoons pure maple syrup
1 teaspoon frozen unsweetened orange juice concentrate
2 teaspoons corn oil
¼ teaspoon pure vanilla extract

1. Preheat the oven to 300°F. Combine all the dry ingredients in a large bowl and mix well.

2. Combine the honey, maple syrup, orange juice concentrate, and corn oil in a small saucepan and bring to a boil over medium heat. Remove from the heat and stir in the vanilla. Pour the hot liquid over the dry ingredients and mix well.

3. Spread the mixture out in a baking pan and bake for 30 minutes, stirring frequently. Remove from the oven and allow to cool to room temperature.

MAKES EIGHT ¼-CUP SERVINGS

Each serving contains approximately: Calories: 103; Grams of fat: 4.5; Cholesterol: 0; Sodium: 2 mg

Channel House Granola

This hearty granola mix is actually much lighter than the original version. However, it is still high enough in calories that it cannot be eaten with abandon.

6 cups old-fashioned rolled oats (not quick-cooking)
½ cup unsweetened shredded coconut
1 cup toasted wheat germ
¾ cup slivered almonds
⅓ cup sesame seeds
⅓ cup shelled sunflower seeds
½ teaspoon salt
½ cup honey
½ cup dark corn syrup
2 tablespoons firmly packed dark brown sugar
½ cup canola or corn oil
2 teaspoons pure vanilla extract

1. Preheat the oven to 300°F. In a large bowl, combine the oats, coconut, wheat germ, almonds, sesame seeds, sunflower seeds, and salt and set aside.

2. In a small saucepan, warm the honey, corn syrup, brown sugar, oil, and vanilla over medium heat. Add to the dry ingredients and mix thoroughly. Spread the mixture evenly in a 10 x 15-inch jelly-roll pan sprayed with nonstick vegetable spray. Bake, stirring every 10 minutes, until the cereal is lightly browned, 40 to 50 minutes. Allow to cool to room temperature and then store in an airtight container. This granola will keep several weeks but is best eaten in the first week.

MAKES ABOUT TWENTY ½-CUP SERVINGS

Each serving contains approximately: Calories: 300; Grams of fat: 15; Cholesterol: 0; Sodium: 69 mg

Roasted Apple Chunks
with Walnut and Candied Orange

This tasty and healthy treat was developed by the Washington State Apple Commission. It can either be eaten like a dessert trail mix, all by itself, or it can be used on cereals, in breads, or even on roasted poultry and meats.

2 Rome apples
2 Granny Smith or Golden Delicious apples
3 tablespoons sugar
½ teaspoon ground cinnamon
1 tablespoon vegetable oil
⅓ cup walnut halves
1 orange

1. Preheat the oven to 425°F. Lightly coat two baking sheets with nonstick vegetable spray. Core the apples and chop them into 1½-inch chunks. In large bowl, mix the apple chunks, 1 tablespoon of the sugar, and the cinnamon, tossing until well combined. Drizzle the oil over the apple mixture and toss again.

2. Spread the apple chunks in a single layer over the prepared baking sheets. Roast for 10 minutes. With a spatula, turn the apple chunks over and roast until just tender, 8 to 10 minutes longer. Combine all the apple chunks on one baking sheet and set aside to cool. Spread the walnuts on the remaining empty baking sheet and toast until lightly browned and fragrant, 2 to 3 minutes.

3. Meanwhile, prepare the candied orange peel. With a vegetable peeler, remove the peel from the orange, avoiding the bitter white part. Cut the peel into long ⅛-inch-wide strips. Drop the strips into a saucepan of boiling water and blanch for 2 minutes. Drain the strips and return them to the saucepan. Stir in the remaining 2 tablespoons of sugar and heat until the sugar dissolves and coats the peels. Set aside.

4. Toss the apple chunks, walnuts, and candied orange peel together and serve, or refrigerate in an airtight container. This keeps for 1 week.

MAKES 4 CUPS

Each ½ cup serving contains approximately: Calories: 106;
Grams of fat: 5; Cholesterol: 0; Sodium: 1 mg

INDEX

242　　　　*Index*